Praise and R
Walking on Water

When it comes to succeeding in business, sometimes it's felt like I was trying to walk on water! Success seemed beyond my abilities and that it would take a miracle. After discovering "The Secret to Walking on Water is to Know Where the Rocks are," I see where there are many, many rocks and options that will move my business and my mission to end teen suicide down the path way faster.

Jackie Simmons
Author, TEDx Speaker, Radio Show Host, Business Coach, and Mission-Driven Mentor. Founder of Success Journey Academy and Co-Founder of the Teen Suicide Prevention Society

Frank's book charts a solid course through the often-choppy waters of entrepreneurship and the impact our work has on the whole of our lives. His own life lessons serve as both inspiration and insight into how to succeed in life, not just work for a living.

Gina Mazza
Author of "Everything Matters, Nothing Matters"

Life doesn't come with an owner's manual. But if you are looking for a manual on how to create a successful business model, Walking On Water is it! Frank's entrepreneurial savvy and gift with words convey strategies for business that make perfect sense.

Connie Bramer
Founder/CEO Get Your Rack Back Inc., author of "How Connie Got Her Rack Back."

The book "Walking on Water" is an excellent guideline to inspire entre-preneurs or anyone who wants to start their own business. The author (Frank Zaccari) identifies hidden pitfalls that have damaged businesses yet provides proven recommendations from experts and an action plan to improve your business.

After 30 years as a successful business owner and executive, Frank Zaccari has lived personal and professional ups and downs. His path has helped him learn a great deal about business, finance, organizational development, people, relationships, and success.

For the first two chapters, Frank begins the journey on the mindset process of starting a business, which arguably one of the most impor-tant elements of any beginnings. Later, Frank focuses on the inner work-ings of the book by discussing these hidden pitfalls that only those who have been in the business for years and have firsthand knowledge and experience.

Frank provides advice from experts; ten successful steps he has used to build and sustain success and balance in multiple industries. He also introduces the TAG TEAM, where he and his partners, including Jay Abraham, will show you where the rocks are so you can walk on water.

The book is easy to read, easy to follow, and Frank provides many factual examples that are well researched. Frank takes an optimis-tic approach while questioning old concepts, such as "best practices," which allows the reader to think outside of the common processes that have failed in many organizations.

Sam Altawil, JD
Author of On The Edge of Effectiveness
– Refocusing HP Efforts to Strength Organizations

BUSINESS *Secrets* *for* WALKING ON WATER

Frank Zaccari

Foreword by Kathleen O'Keefe-Kanavos
Award-Winning Author

WEBE
BOOKS
PUBLISHING

© 2021 Frank Zaccari

© 2021 Cover Illustration by Aljon Inertia

Published in the United States of America

All rights reserved. No part of this publication may be reproduced, distributed, or transmitted in any form or by any means, including photocopying, recording, or other electronic or mechanical methods, without the prior written permission of the publisher, except in the case of brief quotations embodied in critical reviews and certain other noncommercial uses permitted by copyright law. For permission requests, write to the publisher, addressed "Attention: Permissions Coordinator," at the address below.

WeBe Books Publishing
c/o Authentic Endeavors Publishing
P.O. Box 704
Clarks Summit, PA 18411

Book Interior and E-book Design by Amit Dey

Business Secrets to Walking on Water
ISBN: 978-1-955668-02-6
LCCN: 2021910236

Contents

Foreword

Kathleen O'Keefe Kanavos

A business in and of itself is never successful unless successful people run it. People are successful at creating success through their cognitive thinking, reasoning, and problem-solving skills. A viable business is the by-product of someone who figured out the secret to maneuvering pitfalls and uses whatever is at their disposal to create an advantage. As Brené Brown, author of *Dare to Lead: Brave Work,* is quoted as saying, "Courage is fear holding on a minute longer." The result is success vs. failure.

Sometimes the pitfalls within a company can be the employees themselves. However, how do we spot the pitfalls? The lessons learned as the company leader observing employees can become the stepping stones just beneath the business's turbulent waters. Rather than becoming the owner's professional grave like so many wealthy merchant ships dashed upon hidden rocks, discovered pitfalls can become a bridge to success.

The secret to success is how to use those stepping stones to make you appear as if you are walking on water. But, how do you spot the rocks? How do you use the less obvious or hidden in life to your advantage?

Ahhh...that is the secret Frank Zaccari shares with you in this book.
Frank's wisdom is based on personal success, not on a new fail-proof hypothesis or in-depth book-learning based on feel-good ideas rather than real-life experiences. Personal experience makes Business Secrets so magical and vital to an entrepreneur, business, employees, and

managers. The book's simplicity and common sense suggestions backed by true personal stories make *Business Secrets* different from all the other books on running a successful business. *Business Secrets* is not based on the latest business techniques, algorithms, or a recently discovered unique one-of-a-kind business formula. It is real- it is true- it is everyday experiences based on the wisdom that results in proven documented success.

Business Secrets is more than a detailed guide for anyone in business or someone contemplating becoming an entrepreneur. It is an entertaining yet informative experiential teaching tool with a workbook section in the back of the book that can double as an educational syllabus and lesson plan for anyone teaching business classes. Frank fills the book with true stories of both failure and success, making this balanced book unique as it shares with the reader how to build success off of a loss. This book is brilliant!

Yeah, you don't find that kind of education every day.
When a reporter asked Thomas Edison how he felt about his 1,000 failures concerning the light bulb, Edison replied, "I didn't fail 1,000 times. The light bulb was an invention with 1,000 steps. Great success is built on failure, frustration, even catastrophe." Today we take the lightbulb for granted. We switch it on without giving a second thought to all the failures that created the success at our fingertips and beneath which we learn and go about our daily business.

Each of Edison's failures was a rock just below the waters of success. Had he strode on those 1,000 failure successes, he would have appeared to walk on water to all his critics. Perhaps to some people who appreciate that he did not give up after all those failures, Edison still does walk on water.

But, the failures were kept out of the public because stepping-stones-of-failure are seldom celebrated. However, according to Leonard DeGraaf, an archivist at the Thomas Edison National Historical Park and author of *Edison and the Rise of Innovation,* "Edison vowed he would not invent a technology that didn't have an apparent market; that he wasn't just going to invent things for the sake of inventing them but...to be able to sell them. I have to suspect that even Edison, as a young and inexperienced innovator at that point, would have had to understand that if he can't sell his invention, he can't make money."

A good idea alone is not a saleable commodity. Starting a business for the sake of starting a business is not often successful. There needs to be more. Frank writes in-depth about the pitfall of thinking that you can create or run a successful business because you know how to do one thing well. Just because you know how to do something well does not mean it is a profitable business venture. It could be a great idea that requires time, planning, and a team not yet available to the entrepreneur, or the business proposition may be before its time, and timing is everything.

A saleable idea must solve a problem or meet a need; then, people will buy it.
Like Frank, I share this fact from experience based on my successful publishing, promotion, and coaching business. I meet people's needs. My team is in place. Yet, it is only as strong as its weakest team member, so my team is kept strong with constant change, improvements, and adjustments.

Business is an invention. So often, we are taught in business classes the road to personal happiness is professional success. You may have heard the quote originally attributed to flamboyant millionaire Malcolm Forbes, "He who dies with the most toys wins." It means to describe how the person who dies with the most toys like fast cars, big homes, and desirable mates wins. Frank shares his frank truth (no pun intended) of how business success at the expense of personal relationships and bliss is another form of failure. And my thought on Malcolm Forbs's quote is, he who dies with the most toys still dies and can't play with those toys. I hope they had time to play with them while they were alive, but mostly I hope they did not have to play with them alone. And that brings us to Franks's next excellent point in the book balance.

The balance of both professional and personal life is difficult but embracing them both is the ultimate success. If you want to appear to walk on water in both business and love, know where the rocks are and use them to your advantage.

Frank shares advice from a place of personal experience, employs it throughout the book, and in my humble opinion, better advice has never been given.

In *Business Secrets,* Frank does not just talk the talk; he walks the walk.
Viewing failure as a stepping stone to success is very different from Albert Einstein's saying, "The definition of insanity is doing the same thing over and over again, but expecting different results." The primary key to success in both concepts is CHANGE. If you want a different result, you have to try other things, steps, concepts, and people. Change creates change. Even a tiny shift in initial conditions will create a significantly different outcome. Without the ability to adapt and change, there is no hope for a future; and the future of business is always changing.

That said, embracing change is not easy, and just the idea can create a phobia.
Often the idea of creating change in a business or a personal life creates deep fear. The fear has a medical name- Metathesiophobia. In the book *Chaos to Clarity: Sacred Stories of Transformational Change,* I wrote about the Psychology of Change. Change can bring with it a deluge of emotions, from sadness to clarity, to gratitude, and finally, success.

Frank's true stories in *Business Secrets* are from his Voice America Radio Show and are priceless personal business experiences from people around the world. The book shares where the reader can find the links and listen to the show. The guest's tales are built on the complexities of the multiple layers of real-life business experiences that focus on the good, the bad, and the downright ugly. They cross boundaries and speak to us with a global voice focused on cooperation.

Collaboration vs. competition is a keystone to success in Frank's book. He defines the Business Head as profit and the Heart as purpose, and the all too often culprit of failure- Self Sabotage. As Rev. Maryanne Williamson is quoted as saying, "Our deepest fear is not that we are inadequate. Our deepest fear is that we are powerful beyond measure." Sometimes, especially in business, it is our success, not our failure, that we fear most.

Rev. Maryanne Williamson's quote is exemplified in Mel Robbins', *The 5 Second Rule.* "The moment you have an instinct to act on a goal, you must 5-4-3-2-1 and physically move, or your brain will stop you."

Self-sabotage is a lurker.
It lurks in the dark recesses of your mind and waits for your moment of inner pause to lurch forward and gain ground with doubt, "You'll fall down-drown!" Self-sabotage says. A statement as simple as, "I know the secret to finding the rocks for success," is often all it takes to overcome self-sabotage. It is as simple as 1-2-3.

Imagine the true stories and examples in this book as tiny stones dropped into the entrepreneurial pool of consciousness. Multiple stones interconnect to create a new shared space in the ever-evolving realm of business. Their ripples intersect to change the stream of thinking. It may be a new beginning, the start of a journey using life's stones of failure hidden just beneath the water- the secret to success.

Introduction

WHO NEEDS THIS BOOK:

This book is a guide for anyone who is or aspires to be an entrepreneur or wants to run any type of organization. As you will discover many times throughout this guide, success isn't about working harder or smarter. It is not what you know that will determine your success or failure; it's about what you don't know. And, what you know is not nearly as important as who you know. Too many of us sink in life because we don't know where to step for success. We need to know where to step. This guide will help prepare you for what you don't know. The secret to walking on water is to know where the rocks are.

WHAT YOU WILL DISCOVER:

Often, we start a business because we are good at one thing. Well, one thing is not going to be enough to sustain a profession. Scaling an organization and thriving over the long term is something entirely different from knowing just one particular thing. My guide identifies and shares several of the pitfalls that sink organizations. We don't even see many of these obstacles. In my quest to identify them, I met with experts in every area of business and asked them to share their experiences on how to address these issues. I have included ten steps proven to successfully turn around floundering organizations and move them forward in a positive financial direction.

These tried-and-true stories can prevent your professional life from destroying your personal life.

YOUR ACTION ITEM:

You will be introduced to the TAG TEAM, a partnership between Jay Abraham and my company, Life Altering Events. I am forever grateful to Jay Abraham of The Abraham Group for partnering and creating the TAG TEAM with Gaby Ory and me. In a later chapter, we'll discuss in more detail how the TAG TEAM brings value to personal lives and professional businesses. THE TAG TEAM members have all reached a place of success in their lives where they want to see the next generation of businesses thrive. In the addendum, I have included an invitation to send us your executive summary for review. If you think you can make a difference, go to www.frankzaccari.com and download the executive summary application. If you qualify, we look forward to working with you.

WHY DID I WRITE THIS BOOK?

After spending more than thirty years as a corporate executive and business owner, I decided it was time to share some of my successes and failures with other professionals with the hope of helping the next generation of business owners/entrepreneurs to not only survive but thrive professionally and personally.

The sad fact is far too many entrepreneurs, and organizations fail. Why? Well, I believe it is because they are not adequately prepared to navigate the swamp of business ownership. As stated above, most of us start a business because we are good at something, but that something is only one part of running a successful business. We tend to overextend ourselves, try to juggle too many balls – and unfortunately, most of the balls hit the ground.

I found that intelligence, a patent, good people on your team, working 24x7 is NOT the formula for success. You can work like a dog, and odds are your business will not survive, or maybe you do survive, but at the price of your personal and family life. Many of us justify spending our lives fighting and clawing to get "to the top of our mountain" for our families. Then if you have the good fortune to reach the top of your mountain, you turn around and find the really important things, and people in your life may not be there.

Let me give you a small glimpse into my early experiences.

I grew up in a small, hard-luck steel town outside of Buffalo, NY. When, at 17, I realized my dream of playing shortstop for the Yankees was not going to happen, I enlisted in the Air Force and was a military medic at the end of the Vietnam war. Although I was not a combat medic, I did see many things a 19-year-old shouldn't see. I witnessed people whose lives were forever altered through no fault of their own and promised myself that I would not become a victim. My military experience led me to develop a hard-charging Type A personality.

After college, I entered the high-tech world and worked for two Fortune 50 companies before becoming a small/medium high-tech CEO for over 25 years. The **50** companies on last year's list produced a cumulative shareholder return of 71% since publication **vs**. 21% for the S&P **500** over the same span. https://fortune.com/future-50/. These 50 companies alone produced more than three times the return on investment than the entire S&P. I was involved with the "power players."

I was at a senior management level when I got married. Like most people, my plan was that we would stay together forever. We were very happy, at least I thought we were. We had two daughters who were my everything. Professionally things were very good. On the surface, we looked like the poster family for success. I thought I had it all: a successful business, a wonderful marriage, and a beautiful family.

As the CEO for companies that were failing, sixteen-plus-hour days was the norm. I always made time with and for my daughters but was so tired I didn't have the same energy for my wife.

I now realize that as a CEO, the biggest challenge I faced was finding someone, without an agenda, to talk to; to bounce ideas off; to share financial and personnel issues; to discuss how they addressed some of the challenges facing me. Since I didn't see it as a problem, I didn't look very hard for a solution.

I believed I could handle it all myself. I was extremely good at my job; I trusted my judgment and was competitive enough to "win the deal."

I felt an adviser or sounding board was unnecessary and put all the burden on myself. That burden started off as a little ripple in my pool of life, but over time, it grew into a tidal wave that negatively impacted every area of my life.

My temperament changed to the point that even I didn't like myself. I drank too much, was angry, frustrated, and depressed. I was on an emotional treadmill that kept going faster and faster. No matter how hard I worked, it was impossible to keep up the pace.

I lost patience with my staff and dealing with customers, and my business became an annoyance. It was not a pleasant time in my life.

My marriage of 24 years failed. Unwilling to talk or share my struggles with my wife, I guess she got tired of living with someone who wasn't present. She found someone else. And the timing couldn't have been worse.

My wife left the family two weeks before Thanksgiving and just 45 days after my mother died. I had custody of my two young daughters while grieving the death of my mother and my marriage. Everything changed.

Unable to stay in the high-tech field due to the extensive travel required, I bought an insurance agency so I could be a full-time Dad. Moving from a proactive world of hi-tech to the reaction world of insurance for a Type A person like me was like dying and going to hell. After all my monetary and professional success, all my hours at work, and traveling the world, all I had to show for it was a shattered life.

The insurance business was a means to an end. The business did well, and I settled into being a full-time dad. When my youngest daughter graduated from Arizona State University, I sold my company and decided to dedicate myself to helping people and their organizations thrive both personally and professionally.

Because of that one decision, I hosted the weekly internet radio/TV show called *Life Altering Events*. I have since moved the show to ROKU TV. In sixty-nine weeks, I had the opportunity to meet, talk, and work with some truly amazing people. I have teamed with Jay Abraham, Susan Golden, Dr. Marc Porter, Tom Crea, Mark Balzer, Gaby Ory, Julio

Alvarado, Jim McLaughlin, Sam Altawil, Mel Robbins, Jackie Simmons, Gina Mazza, Kathleen O'Keefe-Kanavos, and Nicole Bendaly, to name a few. Each of them shared my passion for making a positive contribution, especially for those striving for success in the business world. My goal became to help executives and organizations avoid the land mines and deep turbulent waters I didn't avoid.

Now, with so many amazing connections, I realized I could help solve the challenge that cost me my marriage and nearly my sanity. It became my goal to create a team of trusted advisers and prevent others from experiencing what happened to me. I searched for the best of the best to invite them on my team and what I found were partners.

For now, I'll sum it all up the same way I do at the end of every radio/ TV show I host and every presentation I give by saying: "The Secret to walking on water is to know where the rocks are." My hope is this book will show you where some of your rocks are so you can amaze yourself and others as you glide to success.

To listen to the interviews referenced throughout this book, please go to: https://frankzaccari.com/free-interviews-sign-up/

CHAPTER 1

Everything You Want is on the Other Side of Fear

Just being ourselves is the biggest fear of most humans. We have learned to live our lives trying to satisfy other people's demands. We have learned to live by other people's point of view because of the fear of not being accepted and of not being good enough for someone else.

Don Miguel Ruiz – *The Four Agreements*

During my speaking engagements, I interact with many people who once had a dream or a vision but lacked the courage to face their fears and take action. They simply settled.

Recently, I spoke to one of my customers who had achieved a fair amount of success in his life. He told me he went back to visit his "hard luck" hometown after forty-eight years. It is a small town on Lake Erie that had never recovered from the loss of the steel mills many years ago. While there, he encountered a few friends from his childhood who had never left. These were people he has known his whole life. They decide to meet for lunch and catch up.

As he drove to the restaurant, he saw what was once a vibrant downtown, now abandoned and boarded-up buildings. Get the picture!

As they sat in the restaurant overlooking Lake Erie, my customer looked out over the lake and saw the old power plant that once employed over 2,000 people. It was now vacant. Not one car was in the parking lot.

As he looked to his right, he saw a large empty field full of weeds where one of the five steel mills that employed over 15,000 people once stood.

One of the friends said, "You were lucky. You had the opportunity to go to college, to get out of here, and build a lucrative career. I never had that opportunity."

Upon hearing this, the man's initial reaction was anger, but he controlled it. He took a deep breath to collect his thoughts then replied, "There was no luck involved. I chose to get the hell out. Growing up, we all imagined that someday we would go to college and become successful. We all had the same vision back then."

The man continued, "When it came time to go to college, I didn't have the money, and my family certainly didn't have the money. So, I made a choice. I chose to join the military. It delayed my vision by four years, but I was able to save some money, and with help from the GI bill, I went to college."

One of the friends said, "We remember when you did that. We thought you were crazy. You enlisted during the Vietnam War. There was no way we were going to do that."

The man took another deep breath then said, "Well, gentlemen, I guess we all have to live with our choices."

Now, what happened here? All these old friends had imagination and a vision, but only one chose to do whatever it took to realize his vision. What choice are you going to make? Are you going to say, "I am what I am, and nothing I do will change anything?" Or are you going to say, "What If?" and have the courage to face your fears?

I recently read The Four Agreements by Don Miguel Ruiz. He wrote:

Taking action is about living fully. Inaction is sitting in front of your television every day for years because you are afraid to be alive and to take the risk of expressing what you are or can be. You can have many great ideas in your head, but what makes the difference is the courage to take action. Without action upon an idea, there will be no manifestation, no results, and no reward.

Remember this, "I didn't have the opportunity" is not a reason or an excuse. It's a choice.

Whether you are a business owner, aspire to be one, or work for an organization, odds are you are not living your passion. If you are like 84% of the population, you aren't fully engaged at work. Pre-COVID, you spent ten hours a day at work with a one-hour commute each way. Twelve hours of your day were spent doing something you did not enjoy. Who knows what life will be like Post-COVID? Now you have an opportunity to press the reset button, to discover what you *really* want to do in life, to make a change. You get to choose whether you are a participant in your life or a spectator.

Maybe you are one of the 16% who is fully engaged. Let's do a reality check. Do you love what you do? Are you excited to get up every morning and face the daily grind? Even if you are happy, I'm willing to bet that some of the time, you still wish you were doing something else, something you were completely passionate about. Be honest.

Did you give up your passion in exchange for the security of a steady paycheck? Did you keep delaying the dream because you just bought a bigger house, and the kids will be going to college in a few years? Did you keep justifying keeping the dream on hold because you haven't yet won the lottery or inherited millions of dollars? Are you holding back because you don't know how to get started? Or are you waiting for "someday" to come? Well, the bad news is that there is no day on the calendar called "someday."

Lewis Carroll wrote: "IN THE END... We only regret the chances we didn't take, the relationships we were afraid to have, and the decisions we waited too long to make."

Is it time to move beyond your fears and have the life that you intended to live? If you are, call me. We'll talk. I'll help you discover the courage to get what you want. That will be discussed in the next chapter.

Stepping Stones for Business Success

1. Be prepared to face your fears. As Joseph Campbell wrote: The cave you fear to enter holds the treasure you seek.

2. "I didn't have the opportunity" is not a reason or an excuse. It's a choice.

3. You get to choose if you are a participant in your life or a spectator.

CHAPTER 2

Do You Have the Courage to Get What You Want

Too many organizations treat heart and emotions, especially vulnerability, as liabilities. The problem is when we imprison the heart; we kill courage. When we kill courage, trust, innovation, creativity, and accountability die too.

Brene Brown – *Dare to Lead*

A s mentioned in the introduction, I'm a radio/TV show host. In the fourth episode, before really knowing what I was doing, Mel Robbins was my guest. For those not familiar with Mel Robbins, she has spent the past decade inspiring, motivating, coaching, and elevating people worldwide. Her practical, no-nonsense advice has changed the lives of millions with a blueprint on how to take charge of your life and conquer everyday challenges. She is one of the most sought-after motivational speakers in the world and an international best-selling author. Mel's inspirational message of hope and positivity has helped so many over the last decade turn their lives around for the better.

In 2017, Mel broke self-publishing records with her international bestseller. *The 5-Second Rule* was named the #1 audiobook globally and the fifth most read book of the year on Amazon. Mel is the author and voice of three #1 audiobooks on Audible and the co-founder of *143 Studios, Inc.*, a digital media company that produces content in partnership with Fortune 500 brands. In January of 2019, a quarter of a million people took part in her free 30-day Mindset Reset program online; and she started "The Mel Robbins Show," a nationally syndicated television talk show.

Her TEDx talk, "How to stop screwing yourself over," has 24 million views. She shared during our interview that the TEDx talk was her first-ever public speaking event.

She said, before the TEDx talk, her life had hit absolute rock bottom. She was staring at bankruptcy, divorce, no career, and virtually no hope. From this place of near hopelessness, she created her now famous *The Five Second Rule.*

Mel said many inspiring things, and two points from her book, *The Five Second Rule,* stuck with me:

> *"When you are stuck, the major task is deciding if you're going to change at all. The challenge is finding the ability, in the face of an overwhelming amount of resistance, to create a small change in your life and build on it."*

Mel Robbins – The Five Second Rule

Now let's think about that statement. The keyword is *if.* Mel didn't say *when* you change or *you must* change; she said, *"deciding if you are going to change."* Too often in our personal and business life we become overwhelmed with a sense of doom. How many times have you heard someone say, "It is what it is, and nothing I can do is going to change the situation?" And then, instead of reaching out to people who can help us, we become paralyzed by fear and uncertainty.

The second point she made was:

> *If you have the courage to start, you have the courage to succeed.*

Mel Robbins – The Five Second Rule

I believe we hold the power to change, improve, and find the strategic partners who can change our life or business trajectory **IF** we have the courage to start.

As I listened to Mel Robbins discuss, "If we have the courage to start," I remembered what one of my professors at UCLA's Anderson Graduate School told the class. He had a unique suggestion for determining who should receive a Master's Degree that boiled down to one activity.

He said: "First pay the fees, so I get paid; then give each of the candidates some money and tell them to walk to the end of the hallway where several vending machines are located. Tell them to each pick one thing, buy it, and when they get back, we will start class. The candidates that can make a selection and return within three minutes should receive a Master's Degree."

Then he stopped and looked around the room. We all looked at each other, then back at him with a look that said, "What the hell are you talking about?" Then, when he had everyone's attention again, he said, "Leadership is about evaluating the options, having the **courage** to make decisions and taking action."

I got it! How can I make major business or life decisions if I can't even decide what candy to buy? I will never forget that lesson.

Now let's get personal. What challenge or dilemma are you facing, and why are you really waiting to take action? Whether in your business (adding employees, a new product line, or finding the right strategic partner), or your personal life (joining a gym, changing jobs, or starting or ending a relationship), if your results aren't what you expected or even hoped for, have you made adjustments to your plan? Your results tell you something has to change soon, but what?

So many people I talk to are in this situation, yet they hesitate to act. Which leads to the question, "Why?"

Are you waiting to see what the latest 'expert' says is the best practice? Are you waiting for new words of wisdom from Dr. Phil or the latest diet program from Dr. Oz? Good luck with that. Every week, there's a new self-proclaimed expert who will tell you something different or sell you a book or a three-day seminar to explain to you why their way is better.

Are you waiting until you have more time next week or next month? Let's think about this. If you don't take any action now, what will be different next week or next month? Are you afraid if you take action, things may get worse? Let's be realistic; how much worse can they get?

Suppose you find yourself in a state of worry, but you're not taking action. In that case, you may be suffering from "Paralysis by Analysis" as you wait to collect every possible piece of information. What we've found is that making minor tweaks to the same tired processes or programs will NOT get the job done. You have the proof. You see the results.

You may have heard the quote by Dr. Albert Einstein, "Insanity is doing the same thing over and over and expecting a different result." And the internet is making it worse.

The best thing about the internet age is we have access to so much information. The worst thing about the internet age is we have access to so much information. We cannot possibly gather, understand, and act upon the daily avalanche of information. There is simply too much to comprehend.

I ask every company and person I work with three basic questions:

1. Where are you now?
2. Where do you want to be?
3. What fear is stopping you from getting to where you want to be?

Usually, fear shows up in one of three areas: not enough time, not enough money, or not enough experience. So, let's look at these three fears.

Fear #1- Not Enough Time: The reality is you have the time. Most of us waste it chasing our tails. You think you are working harder and longer, but things are not getting better. And as your frustration increases, it affects every area of your life. And yet, I have heard more times than I can count, "But Frank, I know it's the right thing to do, but I am too busy right now – this is not a good time."

Are you spending time being a spectator rather than a participant in your life? Are you finding busy work to justify why you don't have time? We all do this – I did it myself. You are going through the motions, staying too busy to change, and making everyone around you, and yourself, crazy.

Fear #2- Not Enough Money: You have the money. You are just spending it on poor options while you hope for an epiphany. While you are waiting and wringing your hands, your cash reserves continue to fly out the door. You may have considered hiring a consultant, a life coach, a fitness or nutrition coach, or whatever, but you probably decided you couldn't afford it. Wouldn't it be better to spend some money working with someone who has been where you are and can help you address your situation with a fresh set of eyes and new ideas? I have found waiting is almost always more expensive than action.

Fear #3- Not Enough Experience: Now, let's look at experience. The fact is no one will ever have all the necessary expertise. Gather the available information, collaborate with your trusted advisers and make what you believe to be a good decision. Then muster the courage to start moving forward. There is a risk to every decision so test the water by taking small steps. You are not locked into one direction. Taking action pushes the ship away from the dock and starts the ship sailing. Once the ship leaves the dock, you adjust the sails as needed. The key here is you worked with knowledgeable people (strategic partners), found the courage to make a decision, and started to move forward. The amazing thing about moving forward is that better times and better people will come into your life.

The people who matter will see you are making an effort and will either join or assist you in your quest. Seeing you take action may also inspire them to keep moving forward, too, and now you have a companion or confidant walking beside you. Better yet, seeing you taking action might inspire someone who is still in a rut. By taking action, you improve yourself, give others the courage to make a decision, and start moving forward. Now, it may be time to mix some imagination into your change. Does that sound like an intelligent next move? We will cover the importance of imagination and intelligence in the next chapter.

Stepping Stones for Business Success

1. Find your passion. If you don't know what it is, we will discover it.

2. Be engaged and involved. Life, or God, or the universe is giving you signs. It starts with a touch, then a tap, then a push, and finally a 2X4 between the eyes. Let's identify the signs you've been ignoring.

3. Be ready to take the first step. Martin Luther King said, "Faith is taking the first step even when you can't see the whole staircase."

4. Stop worrying about how you are going to get there. Start moving forward, and the how will become apparent. If something is meant to be, the doors will open, and you will see the path to follow.

CHAPTER 3

Do You Know What You Don't Know

Far too often, we rely on "gut feel" when making major decisions. Leaders need to be honest enough to admit "they don't know what they don't know." Gut feel and/or making decisions in a vacuum costfar too much time and money. Bring in people who have been there and done that for guidance. Steve Lamoureux

The Fallacy of Instinct: Common Pitfalls to Avoid When Making Design Decisions January 26, 2018

As a small/mid-size business owner or CEO for over thirty years, I have discovered it's the hardest job in the world. Why? Because the rules are constantly changing. Change is coming FASTER than our ability to understand and take action. A new regulation, a new tax, a new ordinance, and everything may have to change from pricing to our business sign. Then there is a new payroll deduction, worker compensation rule, or health care requirement. Once we think we have navigated these regulatory land mines, technology changes, or a new major competitor moves in around the corner or worse – Amazon decides to come into your market. Remember when Amazon just sold books?

"It is not the strongest of the species that survives, nor the most intelligent; it is the one most adaptable to change."
Charles Darwin, British naturalist

"Survival of the fittest is the key," but that's not true. Survival belongs to those who can adjust and adapt to change. The inability to adapt didn't work out well for the dinosaurs, but let me give you two examples of organizations that once appeared to have total control over their market but failed to adapt and change with the times. Maybe it was arrogance, perhaps it was ignorance, or maybe they just got fat and lazy. **Blockbuster** - once owned over 9,000 video-rental stores in the United States. But, in 2010, Blockbuster filed for bankruptcy with almost $1 billion in debt because it failed to keep up with competitors like Netflix, which created a DVD-by-mail service. In fact, Netflix offered its idea to Blockbuster, who rejected it. Blockbuster's poor choice has left only two remaining stores, as reported by the (*New York Times Tiffany Hsu on March 6, 2019*). Now contrast Blockbuster's failure with Netflix's success.

In the third quarter of 2020, Netflix had 73.08 million U.S. subscribers. The subscriber base in the United States accounts for the majority of Netflix's worldwide streaming subscriber base, which at the end of 2019 stood at 167 million. *(source: Netflix subscribers count in the U.S. | Statistawww.statista.com Jan 13, 2021).*

Netflix also moved from DVD by mail to streaming video. In 2007 Netflix began offering subscribers the option to stream some of its movies and television shows directly to their homes through the Internet. (*source Britannicawww.britannica.com*). Netflix adjusted again in 2012, when it entered the content-production industry, debuting its first original series, "Lilyhammer." In 2013, Netflix debuted "House of Cards," which was the first original online-only web television series to receive major Emmy nominations. *(source: History of Netflix Originals - the-bu-buzz www.thebubuzz.com Nov 20, 2019)*

Eastman Kodak – I grew up in Western New York state, not far from Rochester, the headquarters of Eastman Kodak. As late as 1976, Kodak commanded 90% of film sales and 85% of camera sales in the U.S. Kodak did not fail because it missed the digital age. Kodak actually invented the first digital camera in 1975. However, instead of marketing the new technology, the company held back for fear of hurting its lucrative film business, even after digital products were reshaping the market. In his book *"The Decision Loom: A Design for Interactive Decision-Making in Organizations,"* Vince Barabba, a former Kodak executive, offers insight into the choices that set Kodak on the path to bankruptcy. What I found shocking was the section of the book that outlined Kodak's response to Steve Sasson, their own engineer who invented the first digital camera in 1975, who characterized the initial corporate response to his invention like this:

> But it was filmless photography, so management's reaction was, 'that's cute—but don't tell anyone about it.'.

On January 19, 2012, Kodak filed for bankruptcy protection. I recently visited my family in Rochester. I observed the demolishing of many of the Kodak facilities. Its failure created a significant economic hardship for the greater Rochester area. Another victim of hubris.

My radio show, Life Altering Events on VoiceAmerica.com, had over 220,000 listeners in 42 countries. Every week I talked to people who have been through a life-altering event in their personal or professional life. For the past few months, most of the interviews have been about the struggles of being an entrepreneur. The struggles start with leadership and training.

Let me give you an example. Show number nineteen was about **Servant Leadership**. My guest was retired Army Lieutenant Colonel Tom Crea, the author of *Unleash Your Values,* and two separate times led a troop of the renowned Black Hawk helicopters. Tom now trains organizations on how to implement servant leadership to gain a competitive edge. Many organizations are still resistant to this approach. When someone has trained people tasked with making life and death decisions, it might be good to listen to that person.

The first questions from many executives when introduced to servant leadership are: What is it? Why should I care? How long will it take to implement? I can relate; these are the same questions I asked. So, let's find out.

Servant leadership is a term that is getting a great deal of press over the past few years. Is it the latest trendy fad that will fizzle out quickly? Is it just a term for someone to sell more books? We have all seen the signs posted around offices whose intent is to inspire, but do they actually inspire? You have seen them:

- Together Everyone Achieves More
- Great things never come from comfort zones
- Teamwork makes the dream work
- Individually, we're a drop, together we're an ocean

The catchy phrases mean nothing if the words are not practiced, taught, and constantly reinforced. Effective teamwork requires a deep understanding of human behaviors and a disciplined approach to execution. Without the execution, these phrases become a punch line at the water cooler and after-work gatherings.

I had a business owner say to me, "Frank, there are so many leadership models already, is there really a need for another new one?" Let's look at the data found in Tom's book *Unleash Your Values*: In 1998, twenty-three years ago, the Center for Creative Leadership concluded that 40 percent of new management hires fail within the first 18 months; 82% of the time, the reason was a failure to build good relationships. As recently as 2016, they continued to reach the same conclusions. So YES, there is a need not just for a new one, but a more effective and efficient model.

What organizations actually practice servant leadership – not just giving lip service but are actually implementing servant leadership over a sustained period of time? To the shock and surprise of many, one is the United States Army. Now before those of you who served say, "No way Frank. The Army is an authoritarian model. Military leaders are not servant leaders." Well, guess again! From my own military experience as a noncommissioned enlisted person, we were told and trained that situations may occur (although rare) when an E4, a three-stripe noncommissioned officer, or an even lower rank may have to take over, lead a mission and protect the people under his/her command.

Tom Crea explained that a servant leader works tirelessly to develop his or her people and focuses on what they can do for others. A servant leader values everyone's contributions and regularly seeks out opinions. If you must parrot back the leader's opinion, you are not in a servant-led organization.

1. Let others see you serve and encourage them to join you.
2. Make sure they know that you care. People don't care how much you know until they know how much you care.
3. Invest in your people.

Servant leadership philosophy is one in which the primary goal of the leader is to serve. This is different from traditional leadership, where the leader's main focus is the thriving of their company or organization. So, in corporate world language, the traditional model since the mid-'70s has been the purpose of corporations and executives to maximize stockholders' return. This traditional model focuses on the task and not the people. People are often considered expendable or interchangeable parts. It leads to competition rather than collaboration and cooperation within an organization. Now, you might say competition is good, right? For who? Well, in the traditional model, we find a lack of employee engagement and high burnout. Bain and Company's research shows the following (we will address this in more detail later in the book):

- 60% of employees don't know their company's goals, strategies, or tactics
- 80% of Americans are not working in their dream job
- 15% truly hate what they do

So, what is the first step in this servant leadership model? Leadership starts with trust and commitment to values; total commitment to values, not just when it's convenient, and you don't push the values aside to meet a quarterly revenue goal. It doesn't matter what you put on your mission statement or annual report; if you don't stick to your values when tested, they are not values; they are hobbies.

How do you find potential leaders that will fit in this model? Here's an excellent place to start, stop promoting high-performing individual contributors into leadership roles. Because someone is a good salesperson or engineer, they may not be a good fit as a leader. Maybe that is one reason why 82% of the time, new leaders fail because they are not equipped to build good relationships. You are committing self-sabotage when you don't identify relationship builders and do not provide continuous training. Continuous, not the one-week leadership by fire hose training model. We have all been here.

> *Too many organizations provide training one time. It is not the training that has the most effect on improvement; it is the individual coaching that follows it. You must make yourself available to offer advice and counsel as people apply what they learned in real-time situations.*

> P. Leone – Training Industry Quarterly

What are the traits of a servant leader? According to Larry C. Spears, former president of the Robert K. Greenleaf Center for Servant Leadership, these are the ten most important characteristics of servant leaders:

1. Listening
2. Empathy
3. Healing/Humility
4. Awareness
5. Persuasion
6. Conceptualization

7. Foresight
8. Stewardship/Accountability
9. Commitment to the growth of people
10. Building community

Now Tom Crea and the servant leadership community is not the only guest who advocates a new model for leadership and training. Edward Hess, Professor of Business Administration, Batten Fellow and Batten Executive-in-Residence at the Darden Graduate School of Business at the University of Virginia, is the author of *Hyper-Learning: How to Adapt at the Speed of Change*, said:

> *The world is changing at hyper-speed, and we must develop hyper-learning to keep up. The days of power or leadership based on content (I know more than you; therefore, I am better or smarter are over). There is simply too much data.*
>
> *Technology is completely transforming how we live, how we work, and who will work. This shift is big – bigger than the Industrial Revolution because it requires that we humans continuously transform cognitively, emotionally, and behaviorally. A "New Way of Being" based upon "Inner Peace" and "Otherness" is required as well as a "New Way of Working," which humanizes the workplace in ways that enable the highest levels of human performance.*

In other words, the days of, "This is the way we have always done it; My way or the highway; and I know more than you," are over. Leaders must become enablers.

And lately, almost everyone tells me, "Frank, I just want things to go back to normal." We are going to address "normal" in the next chapter

Stepping Stones for Business Success

1. Bring in people who have been there and done that for guidance.
2. Survival belongs to those who are able to adjust and adapt to change.
3. Develop a servant leadership mindset
4. The world is changing at hyper-speed and we must develop hyper-learning to keep up.

CHAPTER 4

What is Normal?

Great leaders are the ones who think beyond" short term" vs. "long term." They know that it is not about the next quarter or the next election; it is about the next generation.

Simon Sinek – *The Infinite Game*

How many times have you heard or said, "I just want to go back to normal?" But what was "normal" is gone. As stated in the last chapter by Professor Hess and COVID related changes, the advances in technology get ready for a new and better paradigm. Standardized, predictable, and repetitive functions will be performed by technology. We must learn and think differently. Let's refer to Professor Hess' view on what normal will become.

1. **Quality, not quantity.** The number of hours we work or the number of reports we generate will be replaced by the quality of what we accomplish.

2. **Adult learning.** The information we know today will be obsolete in 2-3 years. Our ability to learn, unlearn and relearn based on new data will be key.

3. **Not my idea**. Ego is the enemy of innovation. Collaborative thinking, projects, and ideas will replace this thinking.

4. **Open mind.** Be willing to embrace new ideas, methods, and practices.

5. **Address mistakes.** The days of punishing mistakes must end. When people are afraid to try new ideas and models, organizations will stagnant and be replaced. Embrace small mistakes as one step closer to success.

"But Frank, I liked the things the way they use to be." Well, ladies and gentlemen, the only constant in life is change, and the world is changing. Besides, what was so good about the old normal for small businesses.

Forbes Magazine reported Pre-COVID

- 50% to 60% of small businesses fail within three years
- 80% fail within five years
- 70% of SBA loan applications are rejected

These numbers are worse if you're a veteran or from a marginalized community. Post-COVID is only going to get worse unless something changes, and businesses can adapt to that change. Why do we continue to follow a model or set of practices proven to have such a high failure rate? Keep reading.

So how do we create an economic impact amid constant change? Is the intellectual mindset more important than the innovative mindset? Is intelligence important for business success? Absolutely! But is intelligence alone enough? I have the honor of being a mentor and a judge with The University of California Entrepreneurship Academy. These are the ten major research universities in California (UCLA, UC Berkley, UC Davis, etc. - you know who they are). Before I started as a mentor/judge, I was told that as of December 2019, the UC system had 19,224 patents and licenses or pending patents and licenses. Impressive, right? Yet, 60% of the revenue comes from five patents. Five! Not five percent, just five patents.

These are the most brilliant minds in the world, but they have extremely poor results moving from the lab to the business world. So, I asked, "Since you are the best research system in the world, why are the results less than desirable?" Of course, they did the research and came up with five reasons:

1. No Market Need (this is a nice way to say it failed the "who cares?" test)
2. Not Enough Money
3. Not the Right Team
4. Poor Execution
5. Lost to Competition

So, I politely suggested that maybe we should add a number six to their list – They don't know what they don't know.

The intellectual mind required to research, create, design, invent, develop, and test is very different from the innovative mind needed to start, scale, and sustain a business. The Harvard Business Review article of August 7, 2020, by Ashish K. Bhatia and Natalia Levina, raised the question: "Can business schools teach entrepreneurship?"

> "While modern MBA programs offer a host of entrepreneurship programming ranging from formal coursework to startup competitions and incubators, there is a great degree of skepticism around the idea that entrepreneurship can be taught by academics in a classroom. Countless successful entrepreneurs never went to business school — many didn't even graduate from college. Moreover, developing the penchant for imagination, disruption, and counterintuitive action required for effective entrepreneurship doesn't generally fit into a typical business school curriculum defined by abstract analytical models and precise calculations."

There are many reasons why organizations struggle or fail. But, most people don't acknowledge this: many business owners don't know what they don't know and are either unwilling or able to bring in the necessary expertise. Why? This is what I hear most often – "We are smart, and we'll figure it out" or worse, they bring in the wrong people; a fraternity brother or a professor; or a family member – or my personal favorite – "I know a guy!" Ladies and gentlemen, I am an Italian from New York. When someone says, "I know a guy," that is usually not a good thing!

Let me illustrate this point. As a high-tech executive for over twenty-five years, we worked on a project with an Oil Company in Louisiana. Since I was going to be there over the weekend, one of the oil executives said, "Frank, we are going to take you on a tour of the Everglades Saturday." Arriving at the location, I realized that Everglade is code for "Alligator Infested Swamp." One of the oil executives must have noticed my fear and said to me, "Frank, a guide will be joining us in about five minutes." Then he said something I will never forget. "I have lived in Louisiana my entire life, and I never go into the Everglades without a guide for two reasons; first, they know what they are doing and where to go. Second and most importantly, they know where NOT to go and what NOT to do. Every year we have people come down here who don't want to pay for a guide or expertise. They go into the water alone, and unfortunately, sometimes the alligators win."

I hear the same story from many entrepreneurs. They say, "we are smart people; we don't need to pay for a guide; we'll figure it out." So, they throw money down too many rabbit holes trying to piece-meal a strategy. After they run out of money chasing their "I can do it myself model," and they give us a call. By that time, it is usually too late, and the alligators win.

As I said in the introduction, most of us start a business because we are good at "something," but that "something" is often a very small part of running a successful business. We tend to overextend ourselves and try to juggle too many balls, and unfortunately, many balls hit the ground.

Let me give you an example - we are working with a brilliant scientist, and he is floundering. I asked him, "Do you really want to be the CEO of this company. Do you know what it takes to run the multiple projects needed to launch this company, scale, or finance expansion? Wouldn't you be happier being the chief scientist?" He said, "Yes, but then who will run the other areas?"

Success isn't the result of working harder or smarter. It is not just what you know that will determine success or failure; it's also about what you don't know.

What you know is not nearly as important as finding someone who knows what you don't know. Surround yourself with people who have the knowledge, expertise, and contacts to fill in the areas that you don't have or just don't enjoy doing. Focus on what you know and enjoy, then partner or collaborate with a team that has been there and done that. Look for one that's already created, sustained, scaled, and financed businesses.

Now, where are you going to find this expertise? Well, let me tell you. THE TAG TEAM, a partnership between my company, Life Altering Events, and The Abraham Group, have collectively increased the bottom lines of more than 10,000 clients by over $21 Billion. I highly recommend looking for that level of experience if you want your business to beat the odds and thrive.

There is more on THE TAG TEAM later in this book, but first, more on the importance of imagination and intelligence....

Stepping Stones for Business Success

1. **Great leaders are the ones who think beyond "short term" vs. "long term.".**

2. **Your old normal is gone.**

3. **Stop following a model or set of practices proven to have such a high failure rate.**

4. **What you don't know has a bigger impact on success than what you do know.**

CHAPTER 5

Imagination or Intelligence

*Let your mind be open to what is possible. Imagine that things
are within reach by just learning and putting one foot in front
of the other. Where others see impossible, see work, a path,
and blue skies.*

Jon Steinberg

Imagination or Intelligence, which one is more important for success?
Let's look into the statement, "imagination is more important than
intelligence for business success." When I first heard it, I wondered,
"Is this a 'which came first, the chicken or the egg' argument where no
one wins?" Then I read that Albert Einstein is credited with saying this.
Given that Albert Einstein is likely the most intelligent person in history,
I decided that it merited some consideration. So, I looked for similar
statements and found three:

1. "Imagination is more important than intelligence." — Albert
   Einstein
2. "If you can first dream it — you can achieve it." — Jim Valvano
3. "I have a dream!" — Dr. Martin Luther King

These are three extremely accomplished people who used their
imagination, said "What IF," and made a major impact on the world.

Why is imagination important? Imagination creates a vision that people can see and follow. Vision creates action. Here are some examples:

1. Dr. King's dream – and the march on Washington
2. The V Foundation for Cancer Research – which was created from Jim Valvano's death bed at Duke University hospital
3. The Women's March after the 2016 election and many more since then
4. Landing on the moon – President Kennedy's vision.

What do imagination and vision have in common? Everyone can use their imagination to create a vision. Think about it. Vision is not limited to a specific race, gender, ethnic group, religious belief, lifestyle, or political party. It is not limited to the rich, famous, or leaders and is not limited to job titles. Let me give you an example:

I was working with a company that enrolls students into online school at a major US university. This company runs a call center (call centers are today's version of the old assembly lines – long, boring, tedious, and repetitive). The division Vice President asked me to look into reasons why the enrollment group was consistently below industry average and why they had such high turnover. I asked to meet with three people: the department manager, a shift supervisor, and a top individual performer.

I asked each of them the same question: "Describe the purpose of your job." The manager said, "To enroll as many students as possible." That response does not actually paint a picture that would make someone want to enroll or even work for this company. The supervisor said, "It is a numbers game. We talk to as many people as possible about the enrollment process. The more we talk to them, the more they enroll." Again, a less than inspiring answer. The top individual performer, a twenty-four-year-old millennial (and we all have options about millennials), said, "I help people take the first step to realizing their hopes and dreams by guiding them through the enrollment process at one the greatest universities in the world." Now that's vision!

Among my recommendations to the Vice President was to start training this young woman to become the manager ASAP and hire others with her traits and characteristics. To their detriment, they did not heed my advice, and this young woman and several other top performers left this company shortly thereafter.

So, does it mean that if your imagination can create a vision and you have a genuine belief that your vision will inspire action, that you will be successful? Not necessarily. Imagination and vision need direction.

It helps to ask a few strategic questions:

1. Where are you now?
2. Where do you want to be?
3. What is stopping you from getting there?
4. What resources do you need? (employees, funds, sponsors/ collaborators)
5. How are you going to do it?
6. Most Important, WHY are you doing it?

People don't really care about what you do or how you do it. There are hundreds of other companies that do what you do. They care about WHY you do it.

Dr. King's dream is the most impressive to me of the examples of vision leading to action listed earlier. In 1964, 250,000 people showed up in Washington D.C. on a scorching and humid August afternoon. There was no social media or website to confirm the date and time. There was no twenty-four news or talk radio. Yet 250,000 people made it to the right place at the right time because their vision matched Dr. King's. And when he spoke – what did he say? He said: "I have a dream," not I have a plan or strategy or a concept or an idea I want to run past all you people!!! He said: "I have a dream!"and that vision changed the world. Now let's look at how and why imagination and vision are different and why knowing that difference and using it to your advantage is important for business.

Stepping Stones for Business Success

1. **Imagine that things are within reach by just learning and putting one foot in front of the other.**

2. **"Imagination is more important than intelligence."**

3. **Imagination creates a vision that people can see and follow. Vision creates action.**

4. **Imagination and vision need direction. It helps to ask a few strategic questions.**

CHAPTER 6

Best Practice or Next Practice

Best practice is a point in time. It is not gospel. It is not written in stone, and it is meant to be challenged. The best organizations constantly look for the next practice.

Frank Zaccari

"Best practice" is a term that drives me crazy. Best practices are a point in time, and they are not the gospel. They are not written in stone, and they are not forever. I talk to so many people who say, "I am following the best practice for my industry, but I am still floundering."

If it doesn't work for you, then it isn't a best practice, is it?

Maybe you should be looking for the NEXT PRACTICE. Remember what we said in Chapter 3 about the importance of adaptability and change. If you forgot, now would be a good time to go back and re-read it. We'll wait right here for you.

At the end of the day, business models and strategies are just a best guess on how to advance our cause; that's all they are. When they cease to work or when we see something better, we have to be able to adjust. Too many companies become obsessed with their business plan and strategy at the cost of their own business. For the most part, bankruptcy is an act of suicide.

Simon Sinek – *The Infinite Game.*

As we said in the Introduction, the world is changing faster than our ability to comprehend. History is littered with companies that religiously followed their best practice all the way to extinction. For example, during the days when the telephone industry was regulated, the only place you could get a phone was from Western Electric. You couldn't buy the phone; you rented it FOREVER. Now Western Electric gave you some options – the color option was black, and the style options, where to hang it on the wall or put it on your desk. When the industry deregulated, people could choose their own carrier and type of phone. People wanted red phones, and princess phones, and Mickey Mouse phones. Western Electric, however, followed its "best practice" of limited options for manufacturing efficiency. They are now gone.

A&P, which stands for Atlantic and Pacific, was the first of the great grocery store chains that followed their best practice of the same products in every store in the same aisle and on the same shelf. A&P didn't adjust to the demographics of the local population or changes in customer taste. Their attitude was, "we know and have what you need." They no longer exist.

Here are a few more current organizations that followed their best practices to extinction:

1. Silicon Graphics (SGI) and Sun Microsystems – both were high-flying technical workstation companies. In the 1980s and 1990s, both were the darlings for graphic and engineering workstations. In the end, SGI failed for the same reason Sun Microsystems failed. A strange inflection point hit them. A strange inflection point is a moment in time when there is a sudden technological shift that breaks the organizational assumptions of technology-based companies. This is code for stubbornly sticking to your outdated Best Practices.

2. Digital Equipment Corporation (DEC) – once thought to be the company to challenge IBM's dominance in the late-1970s with its VAX "supermini" systems. Although a number of competitors

had successfully competed with Digital through the 1970s, the VAX cemented the company's place as a leading vendor in the computer space. Most argue that it was a failure of the company's leadership to adapt to the changing direction that computing began to take in the late 1980s, leading to DEC's demise. I believe that DEC simply failed to understand that what got you here does not always keep you here.

3. AT&T (MA Bell) – once considered the largest and most powerful company in the world, was unable to successfully navigate the deregulation of the telephone/communication industry. The real cause of her demise may have been her long status as a "regulated natural monopoly." Again, not willing to alter best practices and adapt to market changes led to its extinction. The AT&T that exists today is a combination of the old regional Bells headed by Southwest Bell. They kept the AT&T name, but it is not the old MA Bell.

CHALLENGING THE BEST PRACTICE DISRUPTERS!

Currently, we hear of disruptors in life. We see them on the news where they are considered a negative aspect of change and offered in the light of a negative connotation. Here is a fact. The industries and the survivors are the disruptive organizations. The ones who challenged the best practice and said: "We see your best practice, but what If we did this?" Companies like Apple, Google, Amazon, Netflix, you can name others yourself. These companies decided that the established best practice wasn't the best for them and changed the world.

Apple didn't invent the PC, but the MAC made using a PC easier. Connecting a printer, a speaker to the internet was a snap. Their 1984 Super Bowl advertisement, https://www.youtube.com/watch?v=VtvjbmoDx-I – as of February 2020, had over 1.4 billion views on youtube), appealed to a new generation of customers. Their ads, innovative colors, styles, and state-of-the-art Apple stores made it cool to be a MAC user. Their ads made IBM look old and completely out of touch.

Apple also didn't invent music streaming or cell phones either. Their "Think Different" campaigns changed both the iPod and iPhone from *nice to have* to *must-have!*

Google didn't invent the search engine. YAHOO, among others, was in the market well before Google. It started as a research project by Larry Page and Sergey Brin when they were both Ph.D. students at Stanford University. The goal was "to develop the enabling technologies for a single, integrated and universal digital library," and it was funded through the National Science Foundation, among other federal agencies.

Page's web crawler began exploring the web in March 1996, with Page's own Stanford home page serving as the only starting point. To convert the backlink data gathered for a given web page into a measure of importance, Brin and Page developed the PageRank algorithm. Google entered into a crowded search engine market and quickly changed the language from "searching for data" to "Google it."

Amazon didn't invent online commerce or distribution. They started by making it easy to buy books. We could avoid spending the time and effort it took to go to the bookstore or library. In my opinion, Amazon was selling convenience. They became the masters of convenience with their disruption of well-established industries through technological innovation and mass scale. Amazon is now the world's largest online marketplace, AI assistant provider, live-streaming, and cloud computing platforms measured by revenue and market capitalization.

Netflix did not create streaming video. The founder's Marc Randolph and Reed Hastings, started Netflix as purely a movie rental service. Like Amazon, Netflix sold convenience by mailing DVDs and later CDs directly to the customer. Blockbuster was the dominant movie rental business. The Blockbuster best practice was having the customer come in, wade through aisles of movies, hope they had the VHS movie (yes, it started with VHS) you wanted, rent it for X number of days, most likely return it late and pay a late fee. At times it seemed Blockbuster's primary source of profit was late fees.

Legend has it that Netflix offered its service to Blockbuster, and Blockbuster rejected it. Today Netflix's primary business is its subscription-based streaming service which offers online streaming of a library of films and television programs, including those produced in-house. As of April 2020, Netflix had over 193 million paid subscriptions worldwide, including 73 million in the United States.

INNOVATION OFTEN COMES FROM THE BOTTOM UP

"What If" ideas rarely come from senior management. When Starbucks first started, it was located across the street from the Pike's Market in Seattle (you know the place where they throw the fish). The original Starbucks was in the middle of the block. On either side on the same block was Tulley's Coffee and Seattle's Best Coffee. Three coffee shops on one block. All followed the best practice. Only coffee-related drinks. Coffee, Espresso, Cappuccino, Latte, flavored coffee. NO blenders. Blenders were an unwanted expense. Blenders break down, slow the line, and for "God Sakes" in the 1980s, who would have dreamed people would pay $5.00 for a coffee drink.

As Brene Brown wrote in *Dare to Lead,* a young Starbucks employee in Santa Monica brought his own blender from home and started to make blended drinks, Frappuccinos and others. He put them out as samples. The customers loved them. Starbucks, to its credit, saw the trend and changed its best practice. In the 2019 Annual Report, Starbucks generated 26.5 billion dollars in revenue. Estimates state between 40% to 50% comes from blended drinks. That is between 10 to 13 billion dollars because someone said: "What If" and challenged the established best practice.

Here is an example of a small business successfully challenging the established best practice.
I was working with a tired, frustrated, struggling, and depressed insurance agency owner. This man had spent over 20 years as a very successful hi-tech executive. When his domestic situation changed, he found himself as the custodial parent of his ten and 14-year-old daughters.

When I asked the owner why he had taken over an insurance agency, he said, "In hi-tech, I use to travel over two weeks every month. Now that I have custody of my two young daughters, I can't travel. I have to be a full-time Dad." While this man is to be applauded for putting his children first, his why statement wasn't leading people to his door.

So, I asked him to tell me about the business. He said, "I don't know much about the insurance world, so I asked the local management how do I get this started. They told me, 'the best practice is once you select a location for your office, you market to the zip codes within a 15 to 20-mile radius. There are plenty of people in this radius, and the customers don't have to drive far to your office. You meet and sell them insurance'."

It sounded easy enough, so I asked: "How is that going?" He answered very emphatically, "Not very well. The most profit this agency had ever made was $5,000. The guy before me sold a lot of policies and received commissions, but the agency was not very profitable. Most of the customers want the lowest possible amount of insurance. They constantly pay late, and most of my time is spent calling for payment and putting canceled policies back in force." Then he looked me in the eye and said, "I HATE WHAT I AM DOING!!"

I took a deep breath and said: "If the best practice isn't working for you – then it's not a best practice, IS IT?" He didn't have a vision. He was just following the status quo, blindly following what someone else said was the best practice. So, we set out to create the next practice, a vision that he could clearly articulate.

We changed his "Why" statement (why is also known as the vision statement): We protect our client's hopes and dreams. That is the reason people need insurance, right?

Now, how are we going to protect his clients' hopes and dreams? We changed his How Statement to: "We provide the best possible service and coverage for the fairest price." Not the lowest price, the fairest price. Why not the lowest price? Because people will invest more if they believe what is being offered provides more value. Think of a car; you can buy a Smart car or a BMW; both get you from A to B, but why are people willing to pay more for a BMW.

In neither statement do we mention what he does – which is to sell insurance. Do you know why? Because NO one really cares *that* he sells insurance. They want to know *why* he sells insurance.

I redefined his target market to business professionals with a household income greater than $150K, at least one house, two cars, children, and you drive to see them at their homes or offices. Why? These are the people who have the hopes and dreams they want to protect. The vision clearly resonated with them. He secured the right customers all throughout the state.

Within two years, the agency made $750K in profit. Over the 13 years that this man owned the business, it averaged $400K in profit each year, even with all the California fires. In addition, he retained over 90% of his customers. That is unheard of to retain 90% of your customers in the property and casualty insurance world. Now, why was this agency successful. He realized he could not do everything in his business. Unlike many businesses, he didn't continue to follow an ineffective best practice. He collaborated with someone who showed him where the rocks were so that he could walk on water. Collaboration was one of the key stepping stones to his success, as discussed in the next chapter.

Stepping Stones for Business Success

1. **Best practices are a point in time. They are not gospel and should be challenged.**

2. **The companies that change the world find the "next practice."**

3. **Innovation can come from anyone in the organization – be listening.**

4. **Find someone who can show you where the rocks are.**

CHAPTER 7

The Importance of Collaboration

The best leaders have a continuous thirst for learning. If an organization sees its leader as a learning animal, people are likely to replicate that, leading to greater levels of feedback, insight and collaboration.

John Donahoe

N o matter how smart we are, no one knows everything. As stated previously in Chapter 3, "You don't know what you don't know." We will not be successful in life or business unless we collaborate. Too often, we get caught up in the weeds. We have all been there. The key is how do we get out?

One reason why organizations fail is because inwardly focused people have difficulty seeing the very forces that present threats and opportunities. In other words, they can't see the forest for the trees.

John P. Kotter – *Leading Change*

Your organization is here, but you want it to go there. You are working harder and longer. You have added staff, but things are not getting better. Your frustration is increasing, and it is affecting every area of your life. So, what is the problem? I have heard, "But Frank, it is faster and easier for me to just do it than delegate or train staff." Another one I hear is, "I don't have the money to bring in more staff." I often wonder: "Did you start this business to be a leader or the highest paid clerk at your company?"

Getting out of the weeds matters! You are working "in your business and not on your business." You are too involved in the day-to-day details. Your staff is going through the motions. They are making their problems your problems, and you are allowing it to happen. They go home at five or turn off their PC if they're working from home, and you spend another two to three hours doing their job! Is this going to get you where you want to go?

Leaders need to lead, create the culture, attract like-minded people, establish procedures, approve and/or fine-tune processes, delegate, and hold people accountable. You can't do this from the weeds! So, why not bring in the strategic partners and or relational capital you need to get out of the weeds?

Let me give you an example.

A few years ago, I was working with a group of nineteen youth and family non-profits. They were trying to find a way to collaborate rather than compete. They all have separate infrastructures (information technology, event planning, grant writing, accounting, etc.) and were competing for funds from the same organizations. Many small regional non-profits failed during the financial and housing meltdowns. Many more failed during COVID, and many more are going to fail with the next recession. These nineteen organizations had been struggling for months on how to address this issue. Some executives from outside of the non-profit world were invited to a brainstorming session. After ten minutes or so, a retired insurance executive said, "Sounds like you might like to consider creating a center of excellence where you put specialists from each area in one place to address the common support related issues." They asked him to explain.

He continued, "Back in the day, our support and customer service were extremely inconsistent. Each regional office provided support for their own customers. The best practice at that time was to put your support close to the customers. The benefit was our support teams were able to build a relationship with our customers. The downside was that the regional teams wasted far too much time calling or emailing other regional offices to answer questions that they didn't know or couldn't find the answer locally. We had multiple regional support offices all over the country. So, we decided to move our top support people to one of four 'centers of excellence' locations, one in each time zone. This allowed us to have experts in every area of the business centralized. The cost-saving was outstanding, and we stopped replicating processes. We built a large and easily accessible knowledge base. The only significant downside was our customers called an 800 number and couldn't get to talk to the same person each time." Then he looked around the room and said, "This could eliminate the need for each of your organizations to duplicate every activity by creating a shared service model."

It was like a light went on or the curtain was lifted. An outsider's perspective helped remove the blinders. These were smart, passionate people. Why didn't they come up with this idea? It was outside of their best practice. Rather than looking for the NEXT PRACTICE, they were hanging onto "We have always done it this way." After this meeting, they reached outside of their comfort zone to my friend Sara McClellan, Ph.D., who focuses on collaboration and partnership development. Sara is bringing the strategic partnership expertise in on an as-needed basis.

Collaboration creates a shared vision. Why is this important? My friend Mark Balzer wrote the following in his book *People Principles:*

"A shared vision within your organization inspires action. Great leaders make people feel the vision. Words alone or a sign on the wall don't do it justice. When you communicate a vision, the words need to come from a leader's heart, not from their lips."

Getting your culture right is critical. Culture is far more important than strategy or product, or service. Peter Drucker said, "Culture eats strategy for breakfast." Culture reflects the direction of the organization. It must move people to believe. It must inspire people to make it a reality.

It must appeal to the head (profit) and heart (purpose).
Culture is set very early. Fortune Magazine reported in May 2017 by the time an organization has twenty employees, like it or not, they have a culture. For a small business, by the time you hire your second non-family employee, you have created a culture based on the people you hired, how they act, how they dress, how they speak, how they act under stress. A poor culture creates self-sabotage. How? A poor culture breeds unhappiness. People lose hope. They settle for "good enough." The worst case is the best people often leave the organization.

SELF-SABOTAGE IS MORE COMMON THAN ONE WOULD BELIEVE.

Most organizations die from suicide. Poor choices, poor hires, poor processes, poor attitudes are all self-inflicted wounds. Remember the Eastman Kodak story from Chapter 3? They were the undisputed leader in camera film. They employed thousands of people around the world and were the dominant economic force in the greater Rochester, New York area. One of their own engineers invented the digital camera before the rest of the industry. Rather than embracing this new disruptive technology and expand their dominance, they ignored it. They acted as if it was a passing fad. After all, we are Kodak; we invented the camera industry, the market will follow what we say to follow. Well, you know the rest of the story - poor choices, poor hires, poor processes, poor attitudes resulted in Kodak's self-inflicted wound. Kodak may never recover.

Here is the cliff notes version of another example of self-inflicted wounds. In the late 1970s, the computer industry was IBM and the BUNCH (Burroughs, Univac, NCR, CDC, and Honeywell). The founder of IBM, Thomas Watson, at one time actually worked for NCR. In the late 1970s, IBM controlled the "mainframe" market, an organization's main computer. IBM then created a communication and networking system called SNA (System Network Architecture), a blueprint for connecting to the mainframe. Since they invented SNA, IBM created the devices to connect to the mainframe to extend their dominance further. The SNA specifications were available, and the BUNCH could have used this SNA process to surround the mainframe and increase their market share. Rather than work to surround the mainframe, the BUNCH chose to try to take on IBM's strength, the mainframe. None of the BUNCH could effectively compete with the mainframe, and they faded away. NCR and Honeywell still exist but not as computer companies. Poor choices, poor hires, poor processes, and poor attitudes.

Think about it. Are you struggling more than you should? Ever stop and demand to know why? Too much to do? Not enough time to get it done? Feel like you're taking two steps forward and four steps backward? Do you have to overhaul your staff every two or three years? Living your professional life and, as a result, your personal life is in crisis mode? Like it or not, you've created a culture designed to sabotage your success.

As leaders, we know something is wrong, or we should know something is wrong, but far too often, we put a band-aid on a gunshot wound. Matthew Neill Davis has two statements highlighting this point in his book, *The Art of Preventing Stupid* (you have to love this title).

> *Several analogies/symptoms exist to describe situations in which an organization or an organism is not running right. However, the symptoms are not so clear for your business because most business owners do not understand that their business is a series of interlocking systems, much like a body or a car.*
>
> *Fixing symptoms (the effect) of functional problems instead of addressing the systematic issue (the cause) is inefficient and is not conducive to business sustainability or growth.*

History has shown us a great strategy in a poor culture will fail. Some examples include Enron (criminal culture); Uber (initially a toxic culture which they are still trying to overcome); Bear Sterns, and Lehman Brothers (whose less than ethical business practices were exposed during the financial meltdown). More recently, Wells Fargo, Volkswagen, and Gina Champion-Cain's Ponzi Scheme in San Diego have been well documented. Of course, we cannot leave Bernie Madoff off this list.

Creating a shared vision will help develop your culture. It means things are going to change, and no one likes change. In the next chapter, we will review changing a culture.

Stepping Stones for Business Success

1. Get out of the weeds. Stop working in your business and start working on your business.
2. Work with people/groups to complement your skills and abilities.
3. Your culture is more important than your strategy or products – get it right.
4. Self-sabotage is more common than one would believe.
5. Most organizations die from suicide. Poor choices, poor hires, poor processes, poor attitudes are all self-inflicted wounds.

CHAPTER 8

Changing a Culture

Change is never easy. How do the best managers address change? Model the way, inspire a shared vision, challenge the status quo, enable others to act, and encourage the heart.

James Kouzes and Barry Posner – *The Leadership Challenge*

Organizations don't fail overnight; they often decay from within over time. For many years I was a CEO or senior leader tasked with turning around failing or floundering organizations. Bold and aggressive decisions and actions are needed to change a toxic culture. Even though the employees know the organization will fail unless major changes occur, the initial response is still negative.

As I discovered when I interviewed Natasha Todorovic-Cowan, the CEO of National Values-Centered Consulting and owner of the Spiral Dynamics® Brand, who has created a business that helps organizations make informed change choices,

"Resistance to change is so powerful that when faced with a life and death situation, without a strong support system, 90% of people will not change their habits or lifestyle."

If 90% of people will not change even when faced with life and death situations, what steps can be taken to change an entire organization?

When trying to change an organization, bold moves that reduce complacency tend to increase conflict and create

anxiety at first. Real leadership is the ability to transform these negative energies into positive results.

John P. Kotter – "Leading Change"

Whenever I came into an organization, the first thing I did was to meet with every employee. The meeting had two purposes. The first was to allow each person to tell me their version of "the good, the bad, and the ugly" within the organization and ask each of them what they would do to improve the situation. The reaction to what they would do to improve the situation was usually a confused or shocked look. "No one ever asked me that before."

"Well, you are being asked now. I want to know what you think will work." The second was to explain why things had to change and the process(es) we were going to follow to implement, monitor, and adjust to accomplish the needed changes. I wanted to be sure they felt their input was valued and how their role was important to changing the organization's trajectory. I would also ask them, not tell them, to give the process a fair chance. People thrive in environments of mutual respect and appreciation. Good leaders ensure their people feel they are worth their time and interest.

Getting to know employees personally and professionally, praising them for things they do well, offering guidance, not criticism for things they don't, and helping them to achieve their goals goes a long way in creating trust and loyalty. Trust takes time, particularly when you are changing the status quo.

Like it or not, a person's first reaction is emotional. "Why are we doing this? What does this mean for me? Will it impact my pay or hours? How will my role change? What does this mean for my family?" My friend, Kimberly Davis, in her book *Brave Leadership* wrote:

Brave leaders recognize that they must deal with what's real. What's real in today's work environment is a bevy of emotions that, if ignored, can destroy results. While messy and inconvenient, we human beings can't truly "leave our emotions at the door," and smart leaders know how to recognize, honor, and defuse the heightened emotions in the workplace. They lead through the lens of humanity.

After the initial face-to-face meetings, most people will take a wait-and-see attitude. Many will say they are on board with the program but will just stand on the sidelines and wait for you to fail. They want to see how committed you are to the process. They will be watching what you say, what you do, and how you react to real-world situations. Are you really keeping people in the loop? Are you really open to suggestions? The more you stay on course with your process, the more you explain why you are doing what you are doing, the more you share and celebrate the "small victories," the more people will start to move from "wait and see" to maybe this new program has a chance to succeed.

Focusing on serving the needs of others and not one's own builds trust in a leader.

James Kouzes and Barry Posner – The Leadership Challenge

Let's be real here. Not everyone will buy into the new culture, which is OK in the beginning as long as their actions are not disruptive. The ones who are not disruptive may come around as they see the majority of their co-workers becoming more engaged. Unfortunately, some people will never buy-in. They often become toxic. These people may need to be removed. As Jim Collins wrote in *Good to Great:*

You have to get the right people on the bus and in the right seats. You also need to get the wrong people off the bus.

Let me give you two examples of getting the wrong people off the bus. One of the organizations I worked with was heading toward bankruptcy. They had a good product, but the culture was toxic. There was no trust, and every department was at odds with each other. I discovered the ring leader was the top salesman. He generated the lion's share of revenue, made the most money, and let everyone know that the company would die without him. He approached me and demanded more say and more money, or he was leaving and taking his customer with him. We had two crucial conversations about the need for collaboration and cooperation. His response, "I do what I want. I bring in the business."

Since he was a big sports fan, I explained: "You are like the best player on the last-place team. With you, we are in last place, so without you, we would still be in last place, but the difference is I can bring in several new people who will work to get us out of last place."

After meeting with the leadership group, I terminated his employment the next day. There were cheers and relief throughout the staff after he left, and guess what, the building didn't fall down after he left, and the vast majority of the customers stayed with us. With a renewed spirit of cooperation and some adjustments to our processes, the company returned to profitability in eighteen months.

In another case, I inherited two key employees when I acquired my insurance agency. Both were set in their ways and were dead set against anything I wanted to add or change. Since I knew nothing about insurance, they believed they were holding all the Aces. Several conversations explaining why and the value of the changes went unheeded. At that point, I decided I can fail by myself. I don't need to be paying people to help me fail. Both were terminated and made the same threats as the salesman. While it was difficult at first, the new people bought into the plan, and the agency became one of the most profitable in Northern California.

When you discover a cancer in your organization, it must be removed. Several years ago, I was flying from Atlanta to Denver. I was lucky enough to get a first-class upgrade (remember those?). I had the good fortune to be seated next to Jim Collins. I had read his book *Built to Last*. *Good to Great* had not yet been released. He just identified himself as Jim. We talked about what we did. I said I was involved in turning around organizations, and he told me, "I am a consultant like everyone else." He said, "Let me give you a hypothetical situation you may have faced in the turnaround world. Let's say you have nine employees. Three are superior high performers. Three are average to mediocre, and three are subpar. Where do you spend your time?"

I said, "I leave the three high performers alone, get rid of the three subpar and see if I can elevate the three average to raise their level."

Mr. Collins said, "You are going to fail." I asked him to explain. His answer was, "You spend your time with your top three performers and try to replace the other six with people who are like the top three."

I asked, "Isn't my job to motivate the average or mediocre people to improve?"

He said, "Your job is not to de-motivate your top performers. They are already motivated. The fastest way to de-motivate and lose top performers is to demonstrate that you are willing to accept mediocrity or toxic people. High performers want to work with other high performers."

That answer has stayed with me for over 25 years. Now you should be asking yourself, "If he never identified himself, how do you know it was Jim Collins?" When I bought the book *Good to Great,* I saw his picture and thought, "Oh my God, this is the man who sat next to me on the plane."

After that encounter, the concepts of motivation and demotivation were on my mind – a lot. As I looked into the concept of motivation, I came across this quote from Dan Pink in his book *The Surprising Truth About What Motivates Us*:

Researchers in human motivation tell us there are two kinds of motivation – extrinsic (driven by external factors) and intrinsic (self-motivation). External motivation is more likely to create conditions of compliance or defiance based on the reward. Self-motivated people will keep working toward a result even if there is no reward. They care about making a difference.

You can listen to Dan's Ted Talk: *https://www.ted.com/talks/ dan_pink_the_puzzle_of_motivation*

As we start to come out of COVID, another cultural issue that must be addressed is employees' mental health. Those that were furloughed or laid off, many have lost their health care benefits. They have been sheltering in place, living in fear and very high stress since this pandemic began. Also, what is the impact on employees who could work from home while sheltering in place? I asked my associate, Sam Altawil, JD, about the impact on employee mental health during an interview. Let me tell you something about Sam. He is an attorney and the author of *On The Edge of Effectiveness – Refocusing HR Efforts To Strengthen Organizations.* He is an award-winning Human Resource leader in 2013 as the "Best HR Practice" in an audit performed by the Health Resources and Services Administration (HRSA). In 2015 and 2016, his organization was named "Best Place to Work" by the North Bay Business (San Francisco). Sam said,

"Since we have never experienced this type of pandemic, we have no historical data; however, we know that people are social beings. We need interaction with each other to survive and thrive. People are also creatures of habit. We do not respond well to sudden or unexpected change. When people are removed from their social circles, anger, frustration, depression, and anxiety will increase. Most people cannot turn these emotions on and off like a light switch. It takes time. It takes a constant and continuous pattern of positive behavior."

"Given the starts and stops of COVID closing, opening, closing again, partial reopening, partial closing, we have a vaccine; we don't have a vaccine; there has NOT been a constant and continuous pattern of positive behavior. Smart leaders will bring in or make mental health counselors available. Hopefully, leaders have been having regular 'how are you doing' check-in zoom calls. There is very little positive about isolation. In prisons, it is used as a severe form of punishment. Kidnap victims and prisoners of war are often separated and

isolated in the hope of 'breaking their spirit' or radicalizing their beliefs."

Motivation is less about employees doing great work and more about employees feeling great about their work. The bottom line is: Don't rely on outdated methods and tricks to motivate employees. Talk with your team about the relevance of the work they do every day. This gives you the best opportunity to change a culture. And create great success shared in the next chapter. Are you ready? How do you know?

Stepping Stones for Business Success

1. **No one likes change. Great leaders explain why and then model how to change.**

2. **When implementing change, remember it will get harder before it gets easier. Stay the course.**

3. **Lead through a lens of humanity. People cannot leave their emotions at the door.**

4. **Your focus must be on addressing the needs of others – this will build trust. Without trust, you will fail.**

CHAPTER 9

Creating Long Term Success

The fastest way to de-motivate and lose top performers is to demonstrate that you are willing to accept mediocrity. High performers want to work with other high performers.

Jim Collins – *Good to Great*

A s hard as it is to develop a great culture or change a toxic culture, it is even more difficult to sustain a successful culture long term. Nothing is static—Times change. Situations change. Processes change—technology changes. People or managers change. New people or managers may not have the same passion or commitment. Worse yet, sometimes an organization just gets lazy.

A great culture is self-sustaining. Still, it requires focus, commitment, and discipline. It is not a sign on the wall, or a social media post, or a sound bite, or a statement in an annual report. Your culture becomes what you are, not what you do. People must know what to expect and how to respond.

Discipline, in essence, is consistency of action. Consistency with values, consistency with long-term goals, consistency with performance standards, consistency of method, and consistency over time.

Jim Collins – *Great by Choice.*

The best example I can offer of an organization that first changed a toxic culture and then created long-term success is the University of Washington women's volleyball program.

When Jim McLaughlin arrived as the head coach of the University of Washington volleyball program, the general attitude was, "Poor guy, he is taking over the Titanic after it hit the iceberg." I had the good fortune to work with Jim McLaughlin from the first day he arrived on campus in Seattle.

The volleyball program had been mediocre at best for many years. There was an occasional good year like 1997 when they made it to the "Sweet Sixteen, but from 1998 through 2000, the program had deteriorated. They finished 7th, 8th, and 10th in the PAC-10. Attendance was down, as was the morale of the student-athletes and fundraising. In mid-July 2001, the head volleyball coach resigned. The team was due to arrive on August 10, and there was no coach.

Jim McLaughlin arrived on August 1, 2001. He won a national title with the University of Southern California men's program, and in 2000 he led Kansas State, not exactly a hotbed for volleyball talent, to a 22-9 record, a program-best No. 16 national ranking, and its first-ever trip to the NCAA Sweet Sixteen.

> *Here is the first statement he made to his team: The question to you is this: Are you willing to become great? Moving from good to great is not easy. It requires you to examine and reexamine every aspect of your game and your life. It requires your total and complete commitment. If you are willing to learn and have the courage to change your game, your attitude, your diet, your training, and your behavior outside of this court, you could become great. Coach Jim McLaughlin in the book: From the Ashes: The Rise of the University of Washington Volleyball Program by Frank Zaccari*

To say Jim inherited a toxic culture is a major understatement. The program was in terrible shape. There was a total lack of trust. We started the painful process of building a high-performing culture. We focused on ten steps that had been successful in working with the many different industries.

1. Find the right leader.
2. The leader must clearly articulate the vision.
3. The leader must inspire people to believe.
4. The leader must clearly define what he/she wants to do and what pieces are needed to get there.
5. The leader must select the right people and put them in the best position to succeed.
6. The leader must focus on details and training.
7. The leader must document everything; the organization must operate without key people present.
8. The leader must review all aspects of the operation and make adjustments as needed.
9. The leader must continue to bring in better people than the ones already in place.
10. The leader cannot lose sight of the goal.

We were told, "These steps might work in business, but they will not work here. This is an athletic program, not a business, and you are working with young women between the ages of 18 and 23. Do you really think you can get these 'kids' who have had little to no success with this program to buy in, and even if they do buy-in, they don't have the skills or the ability to execute the plan. You are wasting your time."

As I said to every doubter, "It's my time, not yours. I will send you a picture of Jim and me holding the national championship trophy."

During his first meeting with the volleyball booster groups, a group of about twenty-two people, the new tone was set. The meeting was short and to the point. Jim said, "I don't have and won't have much time to spend with this group this season. I have never had or want to meet with a booster group this large on a regular basis. I suggest you prepare a plan of what you want to do and what you need me to do, and we will discuss it in a few weeks. So, all of you know, my plan is to win the National Title within five years. I don't know what we have this year since I have only met my team once, but we will be better than last season. The team will play with pride and passion. Everyone will see a major improvement in the level of play." Then he left the meeting. The reaction from the boosters was shock and disbelief. "Win a national championship in Seattle, no way in hell." The majority of the boosters left the program believing that Jim was delusional.

Like so many leaders who come into a challenging situation, Jim had a staff (players) whom he had never met and "supporters" who did not believe him. When he and I met, I showed him a business plan to raise money and improve the image of the program based on the ten steps I had used to turn around several businesses. Would this work for an athletic program? We were about to find out.

So, we went to work. Jim changed everything about the program. The way the players practiced, how they ate, the way they studied film, and how they interacted with fans were pre-and post-game. The first year, 2001, was rough. The team won eleven and lost sixteen, but they played with an intensity and passion unseen the past several years.

The goal of the business plan was to generate revenue with as little involvement of the players and coaches as possible. We prepared a situation analysis, a SWOT (Strengths, Weaknesses, Opportunities, Threats) analysis, action, and recruiting plan which adhered to every NCAA requirement. We needed to be smart and target specific donors for contributions and specific players who wanted to be part of building an elite program. We needed to get contact information from the people who attended the matches to build a database. We needed to create a Newsletter and send it to each donor and fan monthly.

We needed to make a connection between this program and the community. We needed a list of equipment Jim needed so I could show it to potential donors. This way, donors could select a specific item or multiple items. We needed to have a consistent story about why the equipment is needed and what value it will bring to the team. Husky fans want to feel like they have a part or a role with the team. At one event, both Jim and I spoke. I held up the list of equipment. Later, a husband and wife came up to me and asked if they could see the list. After looking it over, they said, "We want to do this." I asked, "Which item?" They said, "The entire list." I said, "That is over $10,000." Their response, "Who do we make the check out to." I was both shocked and grateful, and the lesson learned was if you are authentic and show how much you care, people will be happy to help.

We hosted training parties for supporters to learn some of the game's finer points, and we added pre-game chats with Jim for selected donors so he could tell them what the keys to winning were for a particular match.

I told Jim, "As long as the team plays hard every night, these fans will love you and support you forever. When you win the National Title, you will achieve legend status."

The 2002 season saw the team start to win, and donations started to increase. This team, with six freshmen, made it to the second round of the NCAA tournament. In 2003 they advanced to the quarter-finals. Then it happened. The 2004 team went to the Final Four for the first time in school history, and donations increased dramatically. While they did not win the title, the organization had received a taste of greatness and how hard it is to attain. After analyzing the data and determining the steps he felt were necessary to take that next step, Jim made some hard decisions.

He changed one of his assistant coaches to improve the teams blocking. He replaced the middle blocker who started on a Final Four team with a very gifted but untested sophomore. And he moved his best player, All-American Sanja Tomasevic (now the head volleyball coach at Arizona State University) from the left side to the right side. All had an element of risk. All were questioned, but when he explained why to the team and key supporters, everyone agreed.

During the 2005 season, the team was on a mission. It won thirty-two matches, lost only one and went back to the Final Four, and played heavily favored Nebraska in the title match. Washington dominated the match and won the National Championship, one year sooner than Jim had predicted his first day on campus. In 2006, the team again went to the Final Four.

During his time at Washington (2001 through the 2014 season), his record was 357-90 (.799). From 2002 through 2014, they went to the NCAA tournament every year, including four trips to the Sweet Sixteen and one more Final Four. The attendance for the first home match in 2001 was 75. The attendance for the last home in 2014 was 9,000. Five years after Jim left, the new coach has kept many of those principles, and Washington has remained an elite program. Jim then turned around the program at Notre Dame.

Hopefully, USA Volleyball will name Jim McLaughlin the head coach after the games in 2021.

Like Jim, Tony Vitrano saw an opportunity and said, "what if," as we talked about in Chapter 6. Tony Vitrano was the guest on my 20th radio show. He was a close friend of my youngest brother growing up and often said, "I am going to find something and make it big." I want you to be honest here - Have you ever said, "Someday I going to do whatever" or "In a perfect world I would be X." Of course, you have, but most of us stay stuck. Opportunity presents itself to everyone. But not everyone sees or acts upon the opportunity. Why? Too much effort, too expensive, no time, too busy. Tony grew up in a small town that didn't have many opportunities. When he saw an opportunity to improve the experience of attending major events, he left his job and started his own business. As is always the case, he was told, "it will never work. You are wasting your time. You are taking a big risk and investment; what are you going to do if you don't make it?"

We all know wedding planners or party planners who started their own business, but what Tony does is planning on a grand scale. He coordinates events like the Olympic Games, Super Bowls, The Daytona 500, and diplomatic events like the G-7 Summit. This planning is more involved than creating a seating chart or arranging for a caterer.

From the Olympic Games to global diplomatic gatherings, he brings more than two decades of experience delivering unforgettable events on the world stage. His leadership and entrepreneurship in the world of event operations takes the form of intricate planning and innovative solutions for an expansive network of clients whose trust in him runs deep.

Think about all the moving parts that are required to coordinate these events. First, there's arranging transportation, changing traffic patterns in a city, arranging for security in and around the venue. Then there's addressing all the issues that can come up during an event, disaster recovery, and evacuation. (The Boston Marathon Bombing, The Atlanta Olympic Bombing, securing an entire mountain against potential terrorist attacks at the Russia Olympics are just a few examples.) Making arrangements for dignitaries' safe arrival and departures, not to mention constructing and securing the Olympic Village for the athletes. I can't even imagine the complexity, can you?

Tony told our listeners a quote from Steve Jobs that made a major impact in his life:

> *Your time is limited, so don't waste it living someone else's life, and don't let the noise of other's opinions drown out your own inner voice. Most important, have the courage to follow your heart and intuition. They somehow already know what you truly want to become.*

Jim McLaughlin and Tony Vitrano know that great achievements come from great adversity. They saw potential. They identified a plan for success and succeeded, while others only saw failure and then failed. But why did they fail? What do all failures have in common?

Stepping Stones for Business Success

1. Great achievements come from great adversity.
2. Have a plan that you believe in, explain the plan, and have total commitment to the plan.
3. Discipline, in essence, is consistency of action.

CHAPTER 10

My Organization is Unique, Your Plan Will Not Work Here

Swapping your limiting beliefs is critical. Replace doubt and fear with optimistic expectations, which are a significant predictor of achievement. Optimistic expectation will lead to upgrading your habits. We are what we believe we are, and we feed the habits we believe.

David Asprey – *Game Changers*.

We have all heard many self-proclaimed "business experts" discuss how leadership methods and business principles in one area or industry simply do not apply to another industry. They argue, "I am a non-profit, the guidelines used by 'for profit' companies simply do not apply." Another one is, "My industry is so unique that we have to come up with our own set of guidelines." I must respectfully disagree.

After thirty years, I came to the realization that similarities between organizations, particularly ones in crisis, be it a business, an industry, a government entity, a non-profit, an education system, a marriage, a church, or even an athletic program, are strikingly similar. All are failing but are often unwilling or unable to try new approaches. All become very defensive when a new person comes in and tries to initiate change. The majority of the current staff says they are open to hearing the new plan but rarely make a real effort to help execute the plan. They would rather pay lip service to the plan and stand on the sidelines and watch the new plan fail so they can say, "I knew it wouldn't work." The bottom line for organizations in crisis is this – What you are doing and the way you are doing it is not working. That is why new people are being brought into the organization.

While industries and businesses differ in what they do, what we've found is the ten rules or steps or guidelines or principles that we identified in the last chapter that worked in turning around six different organizations, including the University of Washington Volleyball program will most likely work for you too. (You can read more about the Washington Volleyball story in my book *"From the Ashes – The Rise of the University of Washington Volleyball Program."* - https://www.amazon.com/Ashes-University-Washington-Volleyball-Program/dp/145373113X

1. Find the right leader.

This is often easier said than done. How do you know if you have the right leader? Initially, you don't. You do your due diligence, set your goals and requirements, conduct interviews, check references, talk with trusted advisers and make an informed decision. If you do it right, it is not a crapshoot, but you may have to take a leap of faith. For example, after winning the national championship with the University of Southern California Men's volleyball program, Jim McLaughlin could not initially get a job as a head coach for a women's program. He was told women couldn't play the men's game. They are not strong enough or fast enough, to which Jim responded, "They aren't playing against men."

Like Jim McLaughlin and Tony Vitrano, the right leaders can see the current situation and project what it will become. They achieve success because they put in the work and identified like-minded people to join in the journey.

2. The leader must clearly articulate the vision.

If you don't know where you are going, you'll never know if or when you get there. Every leader must have a vision and a plan. Everyone in the organization must know that vision and make it his or her own—the more concise the vision, the better. The plan may be adjusted and modified as situations come up, the vision remains. For Jim McLaughlin, that vision was to graduate every student athlete; to compete for the PAC12 championship, which provides an opportunity to compete for the national championship; prepare players for the US Olympic team. For Steve Jobs, it was to put a dent in the universe, which gave Apple engineers the freedom to design things we didn't know we needed (iPod, iPhone, etc.)

3. The leader must inspire people to believe.
People become inspired when they see a consistent positive movement. The leader must stay the course by continuously articulating the vision and pointing out the "small steps" occurring. Consistency in the message and the method is critical. Think of discipline and focus required by retired Lieutenant Colonel Tom Crea when he led and trained Black Hawk helicopter pilots and crew. They believe what they do save lives and protects the interest of the United States.

4. The leader must clearly define what he/she wants to do and what pieces are needed to get there.
When you take over an organization, one of the first steps is to take inventory of the existing staff, products, processes, procedures, etc. The leader must quickly determine the strengths and weaknesses in each area and have the courage to make the changes that will continue to move the program forward. As I found, turning around companies in crisis means creating connections in every area (staff, suppliers, bankers, investors, customers). This is particularly important with staff. When the leader is clear, the staff is clear and will exceed expectations.

5. The leader must select the right people and put them in the best position to succeed.
The most difficult task in turning around a toxic culture is evaluating and/or replacing the people you inherit. These people were there before the new leader arrived and obviously have some vested interest in the organization's success. Hopefully, most of the inherited

people will buy into the program and be willing to change. Those who change can be valuable assets. Those who refuse have to be let go. As I mentioned earlier, this is a concept Jim Collins described as getting the right people on the bus and the wrong people off the bus. Many leaders will say the most important asset in any organization is the employees.

This is not really the case. What we discovered is the most valuable asset is having the right people. The right people understand and accept the vision. The right people are motivated and driven. The right people are both ready and able to execute. The wrong people do none of these things—the wrong people lower standards. **The wrong people drive away the right people.** Think back to stories in Chapter 8 where the wrong people adversely affected their organizations and had to be removed.

6. The leader must focus on details and training.
There are no small things. Once the leader starts getting the right people on the bus, the next step is to make sure everyone knows what to do and how and why to do it. Many leaders call this falling into a routine; I prefer to call it finding your stride. Consistency is now the key. Constant repetition or practice must occur. The leader, at times, seems like a broken record. Some people call this having a mantra. The leader must constantly preach three things:

1. This is what we do
2. This is how we do it
3. This is why we do what we do – why is by far the most important message

7. The leader must document everything; the organization must operate without key people present.
Far too many organizations rely on word of mouth or the company grapevine to establish processes and procedures. This works if your organization is small with little to no turnover and people interact

with each other daily. Many companies in crisis wanted to avoid creating a bureaucracy, particularly if they came from large stagnant bureaucratic organizations. For many companies, I heard the term "flat organization." "We have someone in the organization who knows what to do when a situation arises." That raises the questions, "what if the person who knows the answer isn't there? Does the operation stop? Do you wait for the person to return in a day or two? What if they get hit by a truck? Worst yet, what if that person has been doing it wrong?"

Let me give you an example. At one point, the University of Washington (UW) and Arizona State University (ASU) volleyball programs were both ranked in the Top 5. Both lost their best player, who were finalists for the national player of the year, to injury. ASU lost fifteen of their next sixteen matches. They appeared lost without their All American. They did not know what to do without her. Conversely, UW won eleven of their twelve matches without their All American. While the replacement(s) were not as skilled, UW knew what to do without their key person.

8. The leader must review all aspects of the operation and make adjustments as needed.
The only constant in life is change. Truly great leaders constantly evaluate themselves. Once they have a good sense of what the market is doing and what opportunities the market is offering, they must have the courage to change and/or adjust.

> *Most leaders get it wrong. They think that organizational productivity and performance are simply about policies, procedures, structures, or systems. The key to real change lies not in implementing a new process but in getting people to buy in and hold one another accountable to the process. This requires Crucial Conversations. – Kerry Patterson, Joseph Grenny, Ron McMillan, Al Switzler – Crucial Conversations: Tools for Talking When Stakes Are High*

9. The leader must continue to bring in people who are better than the ones already in place.

How and why do you find better people once you have achieved success? The answer is fairly basic. If you figured out how to become better, so will your competition. Many great leaders become more nervous when things are going well. As hard as it is to reach a high level of success, it is even harder to maintain. Success also brings competitors attempting to raid your top people. It is critical to continue to raise the requirements and expectations to attract more of the right people.

Think back to the changes Jim McLaughlin made back in Chapter 9 when after going to the Final 4, he changed one of his assistant coaches to improve the teams blocking; he replaced the middle blocker who started on a Final Four team with a very gifted but untested sophomore; and he moved his best player, All-American Sanja Tomasevic (now the head volleyball coach at Arizona State University) from the left side to the right side. Top people will gravitate toward organizations that do what it takes to sustain excellence.

10. The leader cannot lose sight of the goal.

As a leader, the worst thing you can do is relax when your organization is doing well. At times success breeds apathy and complacency, which leads to failure. If you don't believe me, read Jim Collins' book, *How the Mighty Fall,* or go back and read the Blockbuster and Kodak stories in Chapter 3.

It is not easy to build a high-performing culture, but it's worth it. Good things happen to organizations that take the time and effort to build high-performing cultures. They attract high-quality and high-character individuals. Their high-performing culture continues to grow and improve. These organizations have become the dominant player in their industries for years.

Authors Tom Rath and Barry Conchie wrote in their book, *Strengths-Based Leadership*

Strong organizations are magnets for talents. The best people see them as the most stimulating place to be, the place where they can demonstrate their leadership and have a real impact.

Stepping Stones for Business Success

1. Different industries have more in common than they think.
2. Review if or how you are implementing the 10 Steps
3. You will find what you are looking for. If you are looking for success, you will find a way. If you are looking for failure, you will find that.

CHAPTER 11

Is the Under Ground Harming Your Business?

If others don't want to talk about tough issues, it's because they believe that it won't do any good. Either they aren't good at dialogue, or you aren't, or you both aren't. In any case, prolonged silence on tough issues is toxic. Kerry Patterson, Joseph Grenny, Ron McMillan, Al Switzler

— Crucial Conversations

One common thread I discovered in distressed industries and organizations was the number of hidden agendas—internal rivalries within departments, between departments, petty jealousies between staff, managers, executives, etc. Many people "dug in" to their positions or set of beliefs and were unwilling even to consider alternatives. Meetings were two extremes. The first was "yelling matches," where he/she who talked the loudest and longest forced their version of the truth on the organization. Anyone who dared to offer another option was shouted down or belittled. The second was stone silence where no one offered ideas, suggestions, or options because they thought: "why bother, no one cares anyway."

One organization I worked with had an owner who did the majority of the talking and made all the decisions. Anyone who dared to question or offer a potential alternative was belittled or just ignored. Some very good people had left this organization because the owner was the self-proclaimed "smartest person in the room." As the good people left, they were replaced with "yes men/women" who bowed to the owner and attempted to carry out plans they knew would not work.

When I spoke to the owner, he complained that no one ever steps up and takes the lead on anything here. Everything falls on him. I asked him, "Why do you think that is the case?"

He said, "I don't really know. Maybe they are just lazy, and I need to get different people." I reminded him that the organization was turning over its leadership every eighteen months.

He said, "See, even my HR people can't do their job right."

I suggest that he not attend a few meetings and ask the leaders to prepare an agenda and provide a summary of ideas and suggestions.

His response was, "Why would I do that?"

"To give them an opportunity to discuss some options and possible alternatives that might increase sales and improve some of the bottlenecks with your production and distribution."

He just laughed and said, "This is my company. I put up the money. I'm the one taking the risk. We will do things my way."

With that, I picked up the final check for my time, and I wish him all the best. Within the next year, the company defaulted on multiple loans and was taken over by creditors who sold off their assets.

As we said earlier, many people stand on the sidelines and wait for a program to fail. When there is a lack of collaboration, department(s) will revert back to the silo model. In the silo model, a department only worries about what they do and does not actively engage or cooperate with the other entities. This is a form of self-sabotage. One executive said to me in confidence, "When this plan goes down, then I can make my move." I asked, "What move is that?" "My move to take over this department or the company. The majority of the staff will back me since I told them from the beginning that this plan will not work."

I never understood the value of hidden agendas or waiting to make a move. This is a self-fulfilling prophecy for failure. To succeed, an organization must have a shared vision.

My associate, Marc Porter Ph.D.'s research shows that every organization has three distinct areas.

1. Common Ground – people are engaged, feel safe, trust each other, and the process
2. Under Ground – people are not engaged, think "why bother," sit on the sidelines
3. Battle Ground – people have checked out, sabotage, passive resistance, legal action, etc.

Most executives really don't know where their organization fits within these three areas. We have conducted a number of C-Level workshops on this topic. Here is how the workshop "works."

The first step is to explain the common ground, underground, and battle ground concepts and give examples of each and why organizations tend to fall into these three categories.

Next, we ask the executives to write down what percentage of their company is in each area. Here is a summary of what the executives from two organizations, a large department within a major research university, and a law enforcement agency provided.

- 60% in the common ground
- 30% in the underground
- 10% in the battleground

Most of the executives felt this was pretty good. They all acknowledged no organization is perfect, but sixty percent of people on board and engaged is not terrible.

When we surveyed the personnel in these organizations, we discovered a very different story.

- 19% in the common ground
- 66% in the underground
- 15% in the battleground

The executives were shocked. 81% of their employees were not engaged, or worse, preparing for battle. One executive said that couldn't possibly be correct. We told them this is right in line with the available research from Bain & Company, Gallup, Eastern Kentucky University, and Dr. Porter.

Bain reported:

- 60% of employees don't know their company's goals, strategies, or tactics
- 80% of Americans are not working in their dream job
- 15% truly hate what they do

Gallup measured workplace happiness, and Dr. Porter's research measured workplace engagement. The happiness and engagement results were the same.

- 19% in the common ground
- 66% in the underground
- 15% in the battleground

What you bring to work every day either builds or loses trust. How you talk, how you look, how you act on a day-to-day basis matters. In our interview, Professor Edward Hess told me that one day while he was a senior executive, he was walking down the hallway and was so focused on an important issue that he didn't even notice a junior associate who tried to address him. When he got to his office, he received a call from the senior partner who said, "I have something important to talk about; stay in your office; I will be right there." Professor Hess thought this is weird, "just tell me now."

The senior partner came into the office and asked, "Do you know this particular junior associate?"

Of course, Professor Hess said, "yes."

The senior partner then said, "He just gave me his resignation. When I asked why he said you didn't like him, and since you chair the partnership committee, he believes he will never be able to make partner."

Professor Hess said he was shocked. Why did this talented young man think he did not like him? The senior partner said, "You were on the 2nd floor and completely ignored him when he tried to approach you. Now he is one of our best young people, so you are going to fix this right now."

Professor Hess went to the young man's office and apologized. The young man was going to ask Professor Hess if he could get some time to talk about joining the team Dr. Hess was putting together. The young man felt snubbed even though that was never Professor Hess' intent. Professor Hess added the young man to his team, and they worked together for many years, and yes, the young man did make partner.

The important point here is perception is how the other person feels or reacts; even it is not what you intended. While this situation may sound trivial, a valuable asset may have been lost if it was not addressed. As Kimberly Davis wrote in *Brave Leadership:*

> *Trust is critical for success. Without trust, emotions will overpower logic any day of the week.*

In my role as a CEO leading companies in crisis, I heard these far too often. This ineffective dialogue costs you money, revenue, market share, reputation, etc. Conversely, developing a common ground for positive, productive dialogue will give you a competitive advantage. The question is, how?

Some C-Level people I interact with tell me, "This is like feeding the hungry; good concept but not practical. I don't have time for this 'touchy-feely' stuff. Why should I spend the time and money?"

Why? Because high-performing organizations don't just happen. As Dr. Porter tells me, "Developing the civil dialogue to create a high-performing organization is not easy. It takes time, commitment, and tremendous effort."

It is like building a garden:

- You are going to get dirty
- It is hard work
- It is constant attention and nurturing
- Constant review/monitoring

If, as CEOs, we do not address civility, and growing the Common Ground, one of two possibilities is highly likely. Neither is good.

Brene Brown writes in *Dare to Lead:*

> *Leaders must either invest a reasonable amount of time attending to fears and feelings or squander an unreasonable amount of time trying to manage ineffective and unproductive behavior.*

Worse yet, your best employees leave, and other costly actions ensue. For example, employees may file legal action.

Here is some recent data on litigation costs:

- $40,000 Average cost to quickly settle an EEOC complaint internally
- $250,000 Average cost of legal fees
- $50K - $300K Average compensatory, punitive penalties
- 67% of Cases awarded to the plaintiff
- $1M 10% of EEOC settlement
- $115M Average total cost of litigation
- $404M Annual cost to employers for EEOC cases

High profile cases:

- Interstate Distributor Co., Case No. 12-CV-02591 0 $4.8M

- Yellow Transportation Case No. 09-CV-7693 $11M
- Johnson Controls (Civil Action No. 4:11-cv-03506) $62,500

Not to mention the high-profile individuals who have lost their jobs, careers, and reputations, Harvey Weinstein, Senator Al Franken, Charlie Rose, Jeffrey Epstein, and Matt Lauer.

These are frightening numbers, but they just touch the surface. The time lost preparing and defending a case, the loss of goodwill inside and outside your company. The loss of trust. The impact on your reputation with customers, suppliers, advertisers, employees, and worst of all, potential employees.

How Did We Get Here – Power and Privilege

Unfortunately, life and the world are not fair. Those who have privilege don't want to give it up. They feel they have earned their power and position of privilege. While the have-nots claim discrimination and seek the law to "help level the playing field." Strong social movements have led to laws that intended to create a "more equitable" environment going all the way back to the issue of slavery.

Each group that feels they are disadvantaged or do not hold the position of privilege or power will look to legislation for relief. Since 1962 there have been no less than eleven laws passed with the intent to level the playing field against every type of discrimination. Legislation is not a panacea. Legislation provides guidelines. Organizations now have the challenge of translating employment laws into employment practices. So, on top of everything else business leaders have to do, we now have to develop and address compliance training as we attempt to translate employment laws into employment practices.

In the United States, sometime around 1969, in an effort to address the successful implementation of the laws, new regulations were mandated, and we started the era of "mandatory compliance training and corporate governance training."

Does any of this sound familiar:

- Affirmative Action Training
- Anti-harassment Training (California's AB 1825)
- Multi-cultural Training
- Cross-cultural Training
- Diversity and Inclusion Training
- Dealing with Hostile Employees
- Talking "Differences" using Personality Profiles (MBTI, EQ, Learning Styles Inventory, etc.)

Most compliance training is met with massive resistance. For example: "Another compliance training! I don't have time for this! More training to threaten and scare us! This is such a waste of time!" We attempted to make compliance training more interesting and more relatable. We started to use self-improvement Training (e.g., *7 Habits of Highly Effective People,* Emotional Intelligence, Mindfulness). This training focused on "making the individual better, not moving the organizations toward the common ground."

After sixty years of mandatory compliance training, how much progress have we made? There have been some positive results:

- Better awareness of differences (Including pay disparities, racial harassment, etc.)
- A decline in violence against workers (although you wouldn't realize it with the speed of social media, 24 hours news, shootings, and political-related violence)

There has also been a large amount of backlash:

- Increased resentment toward others
- The belief that the pendulum swung too far and the pejorative use of the expression saying someone is being "politically correct."

- Fragmentation of functions (Gig economy–more contractors)
- Underground support groups expanded
- An increasing number of class-action lawsuits challenging systemic workplace discrimination
- Rise of the #MeToo Movement since 2017
- Divisiveness and abrasiveness have become the new normal in politically charged rhetoric
- Black Lives Matter
- Intolerance of others (ironically) grows wider, particularly in 2020

Now what?

Frustrating, isn't it? How much time and money has your organization spent on compliance and self-improvement training? It has become a multi-billion-dollar industry. Unfortunately, making yourself a better person is not enough. The problems are complex; it is time to change the dynamic.

How do we improve civility at work and grow Common Ground? It will not be easy, but the starting point is by reframing and restoring shared values, goals, and culture. For example:

- Job satisfaction
- Trust
- Respect
- Identity around the work itself

The three key questions to build the common ground as outlined in the book *Crucial Conversations* by Kerry Patterson, Joseph Grenny, Ron McMillan, and Al Switzler are:

1. *Do we trust each other?*
2. *What kind of future do we want together at work?*

3. *Are we sufficiently committed to the team's and organization's goals and our collective success?*

Since we live in a "fix it right now world," far too many managers and executives ask the wrong questions, which misplaces their focus. They become fixated with constantly changing the process or procedures. I know I did. This is often a knee jerk reaction, similar to a farmer constantly re-plowing the same field every day. Rather than focusing on changing the techniques again, let start changing the dialogue.

Mark Balzer wrote in his book *People Principles...*

> *All companies are trying to improve their employee engagement, and for good reason, look at any engagement study and the positive impact engagement has on organizational results. Most companies and leaders are failing in this effort because they simply do not understand how to get their employees engaged in the business. Throwing a pizza party is an event and won't get people engaged. The most important step is to define the purpose of the organization, the purpose of the team, and the purpose of the employee's role on the team.*

So, let's go back to the question we asked earlier: How will developing a common ground for positive, productive dialogue give you a competitive advantage? High-performing organizations don't just happen; they have developed a thriving common ground where employees are energized and engaged. As a result, they have competitive advantages such as:

- Create space for more creative product design, process improvement, and strategy development
- Connections strengthen around the work to be done, and problems are solved together
- A decline in an organizational culture of fear

- Oriented less around achieving happiness or demonstrating power and control and more around solving complex problems together
- Dialogues foster shared meaning and understanding
- Revenue, profitability, market share, goodwill, recruitment increase
- Time and money are not wasted preparing for violation management

Nicole Bendaly wrote in her book, *Winner Instinct*:

Negative conflict rarely occurs from issues; it results from negative emotions triggered by an action or words. Negative emotions generate fear in the workplace. People are afraid to be authentic. They are afraid to voice opinions or ideas. Fear is where collaboration goes to die. Fear destroys team culture, eating away at it faster than anything else. There's nothing more damaging to morale than when a team feels like their contributions don't matter.

How do we find our way back to civil dialogue? As my friend Dr. Laura Staley wrote in her book *Live Alive*, the first step is to listen deeply.

Listening deeply is intense focus and attention. It says you matter; I see you; I hear you, and you matter. We listen deeply to understand, not just listening to respond. Once we start listening deeply, understanding, and respecting our differences, civility will become the norm.

What we know about conflict is if people are involved, there will always be conflict. Human communication is inherently imperfect. We don't always use the right word or the right tone or think before we speak. To make matters worse, far too often, we substitute face-to-face communication with emails, or text messages, or slack. Conflict is the natural tension between people attempting to share meaning and make sense of the world through discussion. Conflict is not intrinsically good or bad, but the level of conflict intensity and our tolerance for intensity varies greatly over time and by context. Three examples of intensity and tolerance include:

1. Direct & high intensity – win/lose. We see this in most authoritarian-style management. Not only must I win, but you must lose. It's my way or the highway. The authoritarian leader puts himself on an island. His word is gospel. No one is willing or able to offer suggestions. Without healthy and positive debate, the style will fail.

2. Indirect & low intensity – why bother? No one cares. Groupthink dominates the process and decision-making. Groupthink which often leads to a lack of innovation, comes when the majority of a company or a team all went to the same schools, belong to the same club, associate with the same people, and ultimately think the same way. Hiring a diverse range of employees provides the best opportunity for new and innovative ideas. Groupthink by people with the same backgrounds, education, and interests will lead to stagnation. Arne Sorenson, President, and CEO of Marriott International said, "The more diversity you have, the more you will attract. I have found talented women executives attract other talented women executives to the workplace in a way that I can't."

3. Conflict avoidance – no engagement. Your organization is now in a full-blown crisis. As someone whose specialty was working with companies in crisis, I saw this scenario many times. It looks like this: meetings are silent; people are checking their phones or leaving meetings to take a call; people are taking notes as evidence to file a harassment or wrongful termination case; people are just going through the motions; there is little to no collaboration or

even speaking to co-workers except to complain, and your best people leave.

Let me give you an example:
We were working with a company in the financial market with a fairly diverse workforce at the entry and lower levels (women, minorities, veterans, etc.). One of its goals is to promote from within to achieve more diversity in the supervisor and middle management levels. I had a meeting with the CEO, who told me, "We are not increasing our business with the thirty and under population, particularly with women and minorities." I asked why he felt that was the case. I loved his answer. "When I look around at my management team, all I see are old, fat, bald, white guys. We went to the same schools, belong to the same clubs, go to the same parties and the same church. We can finish each other's sentences. For years I thought this was a good thing. Now the younger people we bring into the organization and train leave us within two or three years, and I want to find out why."

So, I asked, "What are you being told from your exit interviews and your team."

He said, "The exit interviews say they are leaving for better pay and advancement opportunities. My managers tell me it's because these millennials have no loyalty and believe they have a sense of entitlement. They don't want to wait their turn. I want your team to do an analysis."

As we started our analysis, we discovered many of their supervisors and managers were not being trained as leaders. They were good at their job and promoted without any real training on how to move from an individual contributor to a supervisor/manager. Basically, they were kicked upstairs.

I recall a quote from Retired Brigadier General Bernard Banks in Simon Sinek's book *Leaders Eat Last*:

Are you developing leaders in your organization? General Banks contends that too often, a person is promoted to a management position because they excelled in a functional, non-management role. Once he/she arrives in the new management position, they often lack key leadership skills and fail. We often call this the Peter Principle. Is your leadership development plan is based on the "hope method?" Hope is not a strategy or a plan.

We brought in a management training team to design and execute a program for this organization. We stressed that training alone without continuous re-enforcement and without changing the work environment is a waste of time.

Michael Fullan wrote in *Leading in a Culture of Change:*

It does NO GOOD to send individual(s) to training for a new strategy, program, or process(es) if they return to an environment that remains the same. Organizations must change along with individuals. Organizations that want meaningful and effective change must create organizational-wide professional learning.

A second issue we discovered was one particular manager, who was demoralizing and frustrating his staff. This manager had a long tenure with the company and was regarded by most as a curmudgeon, the "get off my lawn" type of person. He was not open to new ideas. He had two very capable women who had the knowledge and ability to make the changes needed to increase the market penetration. When I asked about "the curmudgeon" (who we will call Tom), I was told, "We know Tom is difficult, but he is two years from retirement, so we'll just wait for him to leave."

When I spoke to Tom, he told me, "I have been here for thirty years. I run my shop how I run my shop. If people don't like it, they can leave."

When I spoke to the two young women, they had reached the point of total frustration and avoided interacting with Tom. They added, "We will leave when the right opportunity arrives."

We met with the CEO and asked, "Does Tom have the authority to write a million-dollar check?"

He said, "Of course not."

"Well, his two top employees, both women, are ready to leave, which will cost you a million dollars, minimum."

The CEO asked, "What do you suggest?"

My recommendation was to buy out his last two years or move him to a "paper shuffling" position where he does not manage or supervise people. The company elected to wait Tom out. Four months later, the opportunity arrived, and the two women left to head up departments with a competitor.

Has your culture developed enough where conflict can be addressed through civil and open dialogue? Do employees feel safe expressing what may be considered opposing or different viewpoints?

In their book *Crucial Conversations: Tools for Talking When Stakes Are High,* authors Kerry Patterson, Joseph Grenny, Ron McMillan, Al Switzler wrote:

> *For a successful conversation, there must be mutual respect. Why? Because respect is like air. As long as it is present, no one thinks about it. But if you take it away, it's all that people can think about. The instant people perceive disrespect in a conversation; the interaction is no longer about the original purpose. It is now about defending dignity.*
>
> *The first condition of safety in a culture is Mutual Purpose. Mutual Purpose means that others perceive that you're working toward a common outcome in the conversation, that you care about their goals, interest and values. And they care about yours. Find a shared goal, and you have both a reason and a healthy climate for talking.*

We talked about some of the costs of failing to find common ground. Now let's find out how we can make the necessary connections to build common ground by what we say to each other.

Stepping Stones for Business Success

1. The majority of employees are not engaged at work.

2. Fear and lack of trust are a deadly combination for employment-related lawsuits.

3. Conflict is inevitable, but by creating an environment of mutual respect, conflict does not have to become contentious.

CHAPTER 12

Are You Communicating or Connecting

Trust is, in fact, earned in the smallest of moments. It is earned not through heroic deeds or even highly visible actions but through paying attention, listening, and gestures of genuine care and connection. Brene Brown

— Dare to Lead.

What happened to civility? When did we lose it? Did we ever have it? How can we find it and successfully implement civility for the common good? There is no denying we live in a divided country. Strong opinions, harsh words, misrepresentation of facts, and outright lies have become commonplace. Civil discourse, discussion, and debate have been replaced with name-calling, hostile rhetoric, and at times, acts of violence.

The lack of civility is not limited to the political area. We see it every day in business. Companies that suffer from departmental rivalries (lack of civility or common ground) are 5.82 times more likely to have systemic problems with honesty, according to a 15-year study conducted by consultant Ron Carucci. And widespread issues with honesty can pave the way to the kind of scandals that rocked Wells Fargo and Volkswagen in recent years.

While things will never be perfect, an improvement in civility can give companies a competitive edge. How do we get back to civility? While fear is the enemy of civility, education is the key to overcoming fear. The more we know about people, cultures, backgrounds, religions, races, etc., the better the chances for civil discourse. It is time will stop communicating and start connecting.

Where is your organization? What is the language used most often in your organization? Are you talking or communicating? Do you have discussions or dialogue? The most important question is, are you connecting? In order to have a connection, there must be trust. As we said earlier, people don't care how much you know until they know how much you care.

Is your organization deep in the Under Ground? Let's find out. How often do you hear or make these statements?

- Why is the project so behind schedule?
- Why hasn't this program started?
- Why didn't we see this coming?
- Why is turnover so high?
- Why is it taking so long to fill these positions?
- They said what?

As a CEO, I did my research and hired organizational development professionals to help. I discovered when we spoke and interacted with respect, the organization operated far better.

As Don Miguel Ruiz wrote in his book The Four Agreements:

Fear-generated words create hate between different races, between different people, between families, and between nations. Fear-generated words are how we pull each other down and keep each other in a state of fear and doubt.

I also read in Crucial Conversations: Tools for Talking When Stakes Are High by Kerry Patterson, Joseph Grenny, Ron McMillan, Al Switzler:

When your culture is safe, you can say anything. Dialogue calls for the free flow of meaning. Period. Nothing kills the flow of meaning like fear. Fear stops meaningful dialogue."

Dialogue, there is that word again. I said, "We have discussions all the time about issues. I don't hear hate speech or harassing language. Most of the time, people are nodding their heads in agreement." Therein lies the problem. Discussion vs. dialogue—is there a difference?

My good friend Nicole Bendaly, the President of K&Co in Toronto, wrote in her book Winner Instinct:

> *Discussion, often called debate, tends to be an individual defining or defending his/her position or point of view. The goal is to win. In contrast, dialogue promotes shared understanding instead of individual understanding. In dialogue, no one is trying to win. The goal is to determine a solution.*

My associate Susanna Bravo, MA, often tells me discussion is much like sympathy, and dialogue is like empathy. Again, what is the difference?

Sympathy creates distance

- "I am sorry for you."
- "Let me know if I can help."

Empathy brings closeness

- I am sorry, and I am here with you.
- I am right here to go through it with you.

Another way to look at this is the friend who tells you, "Call me if I can help," but never comes to help (sympathy). And the friend who shows up without being asked (empathy).

OK, now that we understand the difference between discussion and dialogue, how do we encourage and develop dialogue. Again, I defer to Nicole Bendaly, who believes that there are dialogue closers and dialogue openers. What's the difference?

Dialogue Closers:

- "You have got to be kidding."
- "Don't even talk to me about..."
- "No way anyone is going to tell me..."
- "We tried that before."

- "This is a waste of time."
- "Let's take this off-line."

Dialogue Openers:

- "I'm not sure I understand where you are coming from."
- "Can you explain this a little more?"
- "Could you give me some examples so I can better understand?"
- "I hear what you are saying; go on."
- "It looks like we are coming from completely different places; how can we ensure that we really understand each other?"
- "Expand on your idea."

When people feel seen, heard, and valued, you will have the makings of a high-performing organization. This type of culture creates a synergy that leads to more innovation, more willingness to try new approaches and more positive interaction between departments. It attracts/retains high-performing individuals, and like the University of Washington volleyball program, it moves from good to great to elite.

We have talked about the importance of connection and how to identify the wrong people. But what about the right people? How do we find and identify them? My story in the next chapter talks all about Mr. Ms. & Mrs. Right.

Stepping Stones for Business Success

1. **Trust must be earned every day.**
2. **Words matter.**
3. **Communicate with the intention of forming a connection.**

CHAPTER 13

Finding the Right People

To ensure success over the next ten years, build a strong core of people who really care about the place and who have ideas. Nurture strong team players, not heroes.

Henry Mintzberg

I f you are an employer, you know the old normal is gone forever. The days of your staff all coming in Monday through Friday, 9 to 5, are over. Many employees will be remote. Employers are going to need to recruit different types of employees and look for different types of skills. Leadership and management must adjust to this new world.

But what kinds of skill-sets are needed? Too many organizations still have job descriptions asking for a wish list of specific product skills, such as Excel, MS Office, or SalesForce. Why? Those skills can be taught. You should really be looking for behavioral skills or character traits or what are now being called "soft skills," such as integrity, determination, persistence, grit, willingness, and ability to collaborate. These traits/characteristics come from within.

Too often, we look for someone we deem as "naturally gifted" or with a "God-given talent." You know what I mean, the ones who don't have to work as hard to excel. For example, the guy who is the class president, star athlete, best looking, prom king, honor student, you name it he has it, right? But then life happens, and their natural gift isn't enough. They have to grind like the rest of us. Many will fail, drop out, or quit.

Dr. Angela Duckworth, in her book *Grit, The Power of Passion and Persistence*, provides an excellent example from her research with West Point. We all know the admission process for West Point is rigorous. Top scores on the SAT or ACT, honor society in high school and multiple leadership positions in extracurricular activities are a must. In addition, candidates must secure a nomination from a member of Congress (House or Senate) or the Vice President of the United States. The process starts in eleventh grade. Over 14,000 top high school students apply. Only 1,200 are admitted and enrolled. Nearly every man and woman admitted were star varsity athletes; most were team captains. The best of the best, right?

Yet as Dr. Duckworth discovered, one in five cadets (1,200/5 = 240) dropped out before graduation. A substantial number of the dropouts leave in their very first summer during the extensive seven-week training program known as *the Beast*.

As Dr. Duckworth wrote:

> *Who spends two years trying to get into a place and drops out in the first two months?*

This concerned the Army on many fronts, particularly, why and what were they missing so badly in their recruitment and vetting process? The Whole Candidate Score system was failing. One major reason was that often growing up as "the best of the best," they were rarely challenged, they rarely lost, they rarely failed at any endeavor. It was not easy to keep going after failure. We all know people who are great when things are going well but fail apart when things aren't. High achievers are not always the best at a particular skill, but they are constantly driven to improve. Their passion is enduring. They are unusually resilient and hardworking. "They are people," as a baseball coach once told me, "who come to play every day." High achievers have grit.

Back to our West Point example. In July 2004, Dr. Duckworth gave the Grit Scale to determine their passion and persistence to 1,218 cadets. That year, only seventy-one cadets dropped out during *The Beast*. The following year only sixty-two dropped out. Quite an improvement on lowering the dropout rate from 240. Grit matters.

Simon Sinek found the same to be true with his study of the Navy Seals. See his youtube talk https://www.youtube.com/watch?v=zP9jpxitfb4. Simon asked a former Navy Seal, "Who makes it through the selection process?"

His answer was, "Here is who doesn't make it."

- The star college athlete who was never pushed to his limits
- The high school/college social leader who delegated everything yet always took credit
- The strong, muscular "tough guys" who are all about me

The ones who make it have that ability, that desire when they are physically and emotionally exhausted, to find a way to help the person next to them. It is selfless caring and love for your team, for your purpose, and your mission.

West Point and the Navy Seals, two of the highest performing organizations in the world, understand the importance of grit and soft skills. (Soft skills are non-technical skills that relate to how you work. They include how you interact with colleagues, how you solve problems, and how you manage your work. We will go into detail later in this chapter). Yet far too many businesses and organizations do not. Again, I defer to Dr. Angela Duckworth's book:

> The "naturalness bias" is a hidden prejudice against those who've achieved success because they worked hard for it and a hidden preference for those whom we think arrived at their place in life because they're naturally talented."

I had a conversation on soft skills with my good friend Gina Sharpe one morning over coffee in San Diego. Gina has real estate operations in Phoenix and San Diego and has the ability to ask questions and listen for traits or characteristics we now refer to as soft skills.

Soft skills are non-technical skills that relate to how you work. They include how you interact with colleagues, how you solve problems, and how you manage your work. Soft skills include:

- Communication skills – having a dialogue with someone, not talking at them
- Listening skills – listening to understand, not to respond
- Time management – allowing time to think and act, not react in crisis mode
- Empathy – I am here for you

Now, where do we find, hire, and retain these people with grit and soft skills? I believe the first step is a mindset change. I suggest we stop using the term Human Resources and start using Human Capital. I suggest we elevate the Human Capital director to the C suite level. People are the most important asset in every organization, yet the process is often treated more as weeding people out rather than attracting people.

I understand that for some organizations, it is impossible to wade through hundreds of applications for one or two jobs. For others, the process is, "hurry up and get someone in here." I was always taught the concept of hire character and train competence. Character is inherent to an individual, you have it, or you don't. Maybe it is the way we approach the hiring process that needs to improve.

I believe the impetus must come from the top. For example, what function are you trying to get done, and what type of person best fits this role. Second, what other parts of the organization will this role interact with, and what skills are needed for this collaboration. Stop treating each hire with the old silo mindset. The old silo mindset finds a superstar in this area who knows and excels at the job but doesn't care about the rest of the operation. The Human Capital process builds and integrates a high-performing group of people whose skills complement each other and who can and want to work toward a common goal.

The best example I ever witnessed was Herb Brooks, the late legendary coach of the 1980 U.S. Olympic Hockey Team (if you haven't seen it - watch the movie *Miracle on Ice*). When USA hockey was attempting to select the team, they brought in close to fifty of the best players in the country for one week of tryouts. Herb Brooks selected the players he wanted on the first day. He gave his list to the committee, who were shocked, to say the least.

The summary of their comments was: "You are leaving off many of the best individual players."

Herb's response was, "I don't want all the best players. I want the best team." He understood how each role needed to interact and complement every other role. Once the roles were understood and accepted by everyone, trust and respect were created. The organization developed the great chemistry and culture necessary to do what most people never believed would happen; beat the Russians and win the Gold Medal.

I have been told by many people who were part of successful organizations and programs that it is not the work they remember with fondness, but the camaraderie, how the group came together to accomplish something meaningful.

Simon Sinek – Leaders Eat Last

Like the *1980 Miracle on Ice* team, leaders must make sure everyone knows what their role is, why it matters and how it fits into the overall scheme for the organization. This creates trust, respect, and commitment. As Mark Balzer wrote in *People Principles*:

Logic makes people think, but emotions make people act.

Finding the right people also means identifying and retraining the right supervisors, managers, and executives. The people in these positions must "un-learn" the old methods and implement a new style of management that will both attract, and more importantly, retain top talent. One thing a crisis, like COVID, has taught us is that work can be efficiently and effectively conducted away from the office and outside of the traditional nine to five timeframes.

The incoming CEO of Siemens, Roland Busch, made a statement during a recent interview with INC magazine that drives this point home. Mr. Busch said:

> *"The basis for this forward-looking working model is further development [of] our corporate culture. These changes will also be associated with a different leadership style, one that focuses on outcomes rather than on time spent at the office. We trust our employees and empower them to shape their work themselves so that they can achieve the best possible results. With the new way of working, we're motivating our employees while improving the company's performance capabilities and sharpening Siemens' profile as a flexible and attractive employer."*

It is all about outcomes, not hours, and trusting your people. Many companies found that productivity actually improved when people started to work remotely. The pressure of getting the kids ready for school, fighting traffic to and from work, trying to schedule around doctor appointments, school events, and family issues does not create a positive work environment. People do not perform at their optimum level under this kind of stress.

Trust comes down to believing in your people. If you don't or can't trust your employees, then you have a hiring issue with both staff and management. I suggest you implement the Grit Scale, shared in the last chapter from Dr. Duckworth's book, as part of your screening process.

MILLENNIALS AND GEN Z IN THE WORKFORCE

The last area I will touch on is the bias I often hear directed at Millennials and Gen Z. I have heard statements like, "They feel they are entitled. They have no loyalty. They aren't willing to wait their turn." I find these statements amusing at best and frustrating at worst. The fact is, this age group will be the vast majority of the workforce very soon. If you are a business leader, you are the one that is going to have to adjust. Let's take a look at what this age group has experienced. They grew up with

PCs at home and cell phones. They understand technology and use it to implement, validate, and confirm or reject ideas, so be prepared with the facts. When I speak to college or high school students, I know the audience is fact-checking what I say as I say it. Once they know you are authentic, you have their attention.

Here are other facts that I point out to business leaders when I hear Millennial and Gen Z bias. What comes to your mind when you hear the term NASA? If you are my age, the response is positive – man on the moon. To the younger generation, they saw a teacher get blown up on the Space Shuttle. NASA does not give them a positive image.

They saw other things we never saw at their age, such as September 11, 2001, aka 9/11, and a war that never seems to end. This age group saw their parents lose their jobs, through no fault of their own, as businesses moved more and more jobs overseas and repeatedly downsized. They witnessed the housing meltdown where their parents or grandparents lost their homes, again through no fault of their own. They witnessed the financial meltdown where family members lost their jobs. They are living through the COVID health crisis and the associated economic free fall, and let's throw on top of this the intense social issues that have not been addressed. What have they seen that would make them feel the need to stay with an organization for years or wait for their turn? Loyalty goes both ways. I love working with millennials and the Gen Z generation. They are extremely intelligent and passionate. They understand and enjoy collaborating with co-workers. They want to make a positive impact in the world. So, the question is, who wouldn't want employees who are intelligent, passionate, and are willing to work together for the overall betterment of an organization?

INCLUSIVE LEADERSHIP

When promoting someone to management, far too often, we focus on what we can see – individual skills. But individual skills are not what matters. What matters is the interaction between people.

Daniel Coyle – The Culture Code

Finding the right people will mean creating a new normal set of processes and models for recruitment, training, and retention. Finding a new normal means change. I am talking about major lifestyle changes, not a little minor adjustment or a small tweak type of change. We all know that change triggers stress, frustration, and often depression. The fear of making change is known as Metathesiophobia and is in the top third of the most prevalent phobias.

So, what are we going to do about it? As I talked with lifestyle change experts, the term I hear over and over is Mindfulness Training, which I understand is learning to live in the moment. This is much easier said than done. So, what exactly is mindfulness, and how can we learn to live in the moment.

Rather than trying to research this myself, I was recently introduced to Dr. Dena Samuels, an expert and author in building *Diversity, Equity & Inclusion Trainings and Consulting* based on Mindfulness Principles. She is an award-winning tenured professor. Dr. Samuels taught at the University of Colorado – Colorado Springs for 20 years while consulting nationally and internationally.

Dr. Samuels describes herself as "At heart, I am an educator with a passion for increasing your connection and sense of belonging in the world. I am also a springboard to help you reach your own and your organization's inspired potential."

Dr. Samuels writes the following in her book *The Mindfulness Effect*:

> *More and more corporations and organizations are choosing to operate more consciously and to identify as "conscious businesses." Given a seal of approval from B Lab (a non-partisan, nonprofit organization that rates for-profit businesses on social, organizational, and environmental criteria), they are referred to as triple-bottom-line companies: attending to profit, person, and planet.*
>
> *Beyond focusing only on the company's revenue (profit), these corporations pay attention to each employee's needs and even desires (person). They care about the health and*

wellbeing of each employee, personal empowerment, and helping them uncover and work towards their life's purpose to live a meaningful life. Studies have found this increases morale, productivity, and in fact, lowers sick days, which saves the corporations millions of dollars every year. Focusing on the person also refers to developing a diversity and inclusion strategic plan so that every member feels like they belong. The research shows that organizations that include diversity and cultural inclusion in their policies and plans fare much better than those that do not.

When you take care of your people, they will take care of your customers, which in turn, takes care of your business. As a leader, you will spend less time doing and micromanaging and more time actually running your business. What a novel idea!! Staying in the moment matters. Believe it or not, leaders are still people with emotions that, if left unchecked, will become a problem. I asked Dr. Samuels to give us a simple Mindfulness exercise. You can do this yourself right now she calls it a Ten Second Vacation:

- Inhale very deeply from your diaphragm for four seconds.
- Exhale for six seconds.
- The act of exhaling longer than inhaling calms the parasympathetic nervous system, which in turn lowers the Cortisol (stress) level. Now you should feel calmer. OK, now take the Ten Second Vacation again – for those of you who did not do it – do it now.

To attract the new generation of employees, organizations will have to develop and implement environmental standards and practices. Simply having a recycle bin will no longer be good enough. As Dr. Samuels explains:

The third bottom-line is a focus on our connection to the earth (planet). These companies research and develop sustainable practices because they take into account their impact on the earth for future generations. Some of the companies that are not only succeeding but soaring using this model are Seventh Generation, Method Home, DHL, Patagonia, among others. More will follow suit if we demand that they do.

We are on the precipice of a new frontier. It will take mindful leadership that highlights inclusive excellence to leave the planet and its inhabitants in better shape than it was when we got here. It will take mindful leaders:

- *who know to respond rather than to react to any given situation;*
- *who excel at mindful listening by using Beginner's Mind to hear and appreciate new and different voices than have traditionally been allowed to speak;*
- *and who operate in mindful awareness of our impact on the earth.*

If leaders and organizations follow the advice of Roland Busch and Dr. Dena Samuels, I believe we will see unprecedented growth in innovation, discovery, and progress.

Stepping Stones for Business Success

1. **A new recruiting model based on character traits and soft skills is needed.**
2. **Look for people with passion and persistence (Grit).**
3. **Nurture strong team players, not heroes.**

CHAPTER 14

The New Breed of Innovators

"Thinking innovatively is one thing. Building an innovative team — one willing to volunteer ideas and take risks — is another. Embracing innovation adds value company-wide, from eliminating inefficiencies and attracting top talent to increasing customer satisfaction and, ultimately, growing profits."Geralyn Hurd, a partner at the accounting, consulting, and technology firm Crowe.

Grammy Award winner Bruno Mars has a great line in his hit song, "Uptown Funk." The line is, *"Don't Believe Me? Just Watch!"* This line makes me think of all the people who have been counted out, disregarded, or marginalized because they didn't follow the "established set of rules." They have been called names like strange, odd, different, or a little off. A kinder statement is they are a free spirit.

Well, many of these free spirits create their own path, dance to their own music, trust, and follow their own set beliefs. They are confident, not arrogant, in their ability; they are risk-takers but not reckless.

These free spirits see opportunities where others see problems. They study and research why there is an issue with the current method, collaborate with other like-minded people to determine if and how a different approach will improve the situation, and then most importantly, they take action. These free spirits are innovators or, a new term, designers in the truest sense of the word.

I love the term designers. I recently read the book: *Designing Your Life* by Bill Burnett and Dave Evans, who wrote:

> *Designers imagine things that don't yet exist, and then they build them, and the world changes. Designers believe in radical collaboration.*

In other words, they seek organizations like THE TAG TEAM to develop strategic alliances and relational capital to investigate and try to do what hasn't been done or designed in a completely new way to drastically improve a process or industry. They look at the established best practice and often say, "I see what you are doing, but what if we did this?"

Don't believe me; look at Starbucks, Apple, Google, Amazon. They didn't invent coffee shops, or technology, or search engines, or logistics. What they did was design a better, more intuitive, and convenient customer experience. They changed the world.

David Asprey wrote in his book *Game Changers;*

> *Authority figures are created to protect the status quo. Being an innovator requires you to think differently. Stagnation and fear are the enemy of innovation. Fear of failure causes failure.*

Designers aren't afraid of failure. In fact, they view what most of us call failure as one step closer to success. They start the project, test and challenge the progress, make adjustments and keep moving forward. They don't worry about perfection because perfection never happens. Instead of perfection, they practice reflection and redirection with the goal of continuous improvement. Unlike many major corporations or established organizations, they don't milk their product or solution. Why is this important? I have been involved with far too many people or organizations that once they find initial success, they get lazy. They turn their focus to attacking their competitors or hyping themselves with marketing/branding propaganda.

Our free-spirited innovators/designers continue to make their product or solution better to the point where there is no other viable alternative. Their solutions are not just what the customers do or buy; it is what they are. For example, Harley Davidson customers are Harley Davidson. They will wait longer and pay more because they are Harley Owners and are a member of the Harley Owners Group, a.k.a. HOGs. There is no other option. The same is true with Apple, from Macs to iPhones, to iPods to "iEverything." Their customers will continue to follow them.

The new breed of innovators does not accept limits or feel compelled to comply with established best practices. They constantly look for a better way. My long-time friend Frannie Matthews, President and CEO at Colorado Technology Association, shared an actual story about one of her daughters who has a degree in business analytics in an article she wrote named: *"Mom, I just eliminated my own job." The Best Mother's Day Present Ever.*

> *A few weeks ago, I received a text from my daughter, "Please call. Not urgent, but important. Need advice." She needs me AND my advice! In an attempt to hide my neediness to be needed, I waited a full two minutes before asking Siri to place the call.*
>
> *"Hi, what's up, Sweetie?" She began to tell me about her job and about how she was doing a lot of repetitive tasks. "I think I can write an algorithm that would eliminate much of the work I do. If I do, they might not need me anymore." I tried to stay calm, but I was nothing short of giddy. "Do it! Put together your plan, share it with your manager, and do it! They will need you more than ever because that's EXACTLY what every employer needs."*

I'll summarize the rest of the conversation (i.e., lecture)

1. Continuously looking for better ways of accomplishing work is a good thing. If something doesn't make sense or is inefficient,

propose a thoughtful solution. Creativity, execution, feedback, and iteration are the cornerstones of success in this dynamic world.

2. Eliminate inefficiency, or someone else will do it for you. I have one word: Uber. I have a second word: Airbnb.

3. Don't do work that a robot or computer can do. Big Data is getting bigger, robots and computers are getting smarter, and infrastructure is getting less expensive. These trends will change the skills required in many fields. Jobs will be eliminated. Here's the good news, new jobs will appear. Lots of new jobs. To quote Wayne Gretzky, "A great .... player plays where the puck is going to be." Be alert and find the gaps.

4. Listen to your mother. No further explanation is required.

> Epilogue: She did write the algorithm, she didn't get fired, she's doing interesting work, and now knows who Wayne Gretzky is. Life is good.

Young innovative and talented people like Frannie's daughter are what every organization needs. They look for and find solutions. They have what Dr. Carol Dweck calls an open mindset.

> *The people we most admire have character, heart, and the mind of a champion. They possess a growth mindset that focuses on self-development, self-motivation, and responsibility.*
>
> Carol S. Dweck – *Mindset: The New Psychology of Success.*

You may have heard the quote by Carroll Bryant —

> 'Some people make things happen. Some people watch things happen. And then there are those who wonder, 'What the hell just happened?'

These free-spirited innovators/designers are the people who make a major impact in the world or their industry. They believe none of us are in this alone. The secret to walking on water is to know where the rocks are, and they are finding the rocks.

You know what and who I am talking about. I am willing to bet I am talking about you.

If this is you – then connect with us. THE TAG TEAM is looking for you.

Stepping Stones for Business Success

1. **Don't believe me, just watch.**

2. **Find opportunities where others find problems.**

3. **Creativity, execution, feedback, and iteration are the cornerstones of success in this dynamic world.**

CHAPTER 15

Press the Reset Button

When emotions are high, intelligence is low!

Nicole Bendaly – *Winner Instinct*

Hard times are going to happen in life and business. No matter what life throws our way, we have the power and the ability to overcome any and every obstacle. Think about what we have experienced and survived just since 2001:

1. September 11
2. A never-ending war
3. The financial meltdown
4. The housing crisis
5. Three major recessions
6. Corporate downsizing
7. Outsourcing jobs overseas
8. Trade Wars
9. Two impeachments
10. Attack on the Capital
11. COVID
12. Shelter in place
13. Furloughed from work or your job eliminated, or your business failed

How we act, not react, during hard times will determine our fate. Great achievements come from great adversity. There are so many opportunities during this time of adversity if you know where to look and how to structure the process.

As we learned with COVID-19, the financial meltdown and the other crisis listed above is our world will be turned upside down to where we frequently find ourselves in uncharted territory. Most of our businesses were closed for a period of time, some for a very long time, and many never reopened. If we were lucky, our staff and we could work from home. Social distancing, a word never hear before February 2020, is now a standard component of nearly every conversation. We are all going through the same "Life Altering Event" at the same time. As I tell my radio and TV audience every week: "Life altering events present us with opportunities to seize the moment and make a difference in our life. They are a fork in the road where we have a choice. We can choose to fall apart, or we can choose to find the courage, pick up the pieces, deal with our grief and start moving forward toward better times and better people. Always remember this, it is never too late to have the life you want and deserve."

My associate Jay Abraham often says, "There are many ethical opportunities available during hard times." I stress the word ethical. There are more opportunities to collaborate with other companies. Some are through strategic alliances, merging or acquiring assets, offering a new service, pivoting to an entirely new business, or changing your business model. Let me give you one example. COVID hit restaurants particularly hard. Since many fine dining places are not like fast food with drive-throughs, they had to get creative. One suggestion was to contact the customers via email or phone to thank them for their business and let them know they could still enjoy great meals during the quarantine. The message also stated something to the effect, 'Tuesday, Wednesday and Thursday we will be preparing a special meal (particular dish). Call or email us your order by X date. We will prepare your meal. The delivery to your home will be on us. We appreciate your business and look forward to seeing you in person as soon as possible.

Wow, what a great plan for the restaurants that acted on the suggestion. The customers feel appreciated while they are staying home and are most likely getting tired of trying to cook every day or eating fast food delivery. The restaurant stayed on top of mind with their customers and received some revenue. They were able to maintain their key employees, but what was most important is when customers were able to dine in again, they went back and brought friends and family.

So now what? Consider this, during hard times; it is the perfect time to press the reset button and look at our business and our life. As business leaders, we are always thinking about things we can do better, how we can improve our processes, and how we can improve our customer's experience.

Unfortunately, we rarely find time to sit down and reflect on the hundreds of thoughts racing through our minds. Our staff, which is closer to the situation, can't offer suggestions because they are overwhelmed with their day-to-day activities. Well, now you have the time – so let's use it wisely. Turn off the news, walk to a park or the ocean, or whatever place gives you a sense of peace. Keep a safe social distance from others, take a deep breath and reflect on these four points:

1. **Why are we doing what we are doing**? It is more than just making a living. What value do we bring to the world and our customers? Are we doing things the best way for our customers, or what is easiest for us? Be honest.

2. **How do we do what we do**? Talk or email your staff. Ask them how we can make this process better, more efficient, and more effective. You may be shocked to hear their ideas. They may be living with an ineffective process because "it is what it is," a term I truly dislike.

3. **Empower your staff to execute their idea**. When people have "skin" in the game, when their input is valued enough to implement, they will give a level of effort you never saw before.

They become the expert in their area. You may even develop "The Next Practice" rather than following the old best practice that is past its prime. I was always taught that if I am the smartest person in the room, I am in the wrong room.

4. **Focus on continuous improvement**. As we stated in The New Breed of Innovator chapter, don't be like most organizations who try to "milk" a product or solution rather than continuing to improve. When your customers and staff see that you are totally committed to improving every aspect of your business, you will become the "go-to" company. Your customers and staff will not even consider an alternative because they know you are meeting their needs today and will be there with even better solutions in the future.

It doesn't matter what industry you are in because these points are Universal.

And . . .the more we try to control things, the less control we actually have. At the end of my weekly radio and TV show, I often say, "None of us are in this alone. The secret to walking on water is knowing where the rocks are." (and for that, we often need another's perspective)

ACT... DON'T REACT.

Knee-jerk reactions to a situation are usually wrong choices because they tend to be emotional rather than rational. As stated earlier, when emotions are high, intelligence is low. I have witnessed many Fortune 500 companies and small businesses react and cut staff and marketing. Not the best move. While the situation may evolve to where you have to make those cuts, they should not be step #1.

I suggest your first step is to explain the situation to your staff and lay out a plan and ask for input, as mentioned above. Your staff already knows something is wrong, and human nature is to create a worst-case scenario when facts are not forthcoming.

Brene Brown wrote in *Dare to Lead:*

Confabulation has a really great and subtle definition: A confabulation is a lie told honestly.

To confabulate is to replace missing information with something false that we believe to be true.

Brene Brown – *Dare to Lead.*

Think of all the BOTs we see on social media. For those unfamiliar with BOTS, they are a profile on a social media platform that is automatically programmed to generate messages, follow accounts, reply to or share particular hashtags, usually using Machine Learning.

You need your staff to keep things moving. Your best people will rise to the occasion, and they are a great source to keep your customers calm. When your staff is panicking, it comes across to your customers, and during hard times, the last thing you need is for your customers to start looking elsewhere.

Continue to market your business during hard times. In an August 14, 2020 article in the Harvard Business Review, Nirmalya Kumar and Koen Pauwels wrote *Don't Cut Your Marketing Budget in a Recession.*

Companies that have bounced back most strongly from previous recessions usually did not cut their marketing spending, and in many cases, actually increased it. But they did change what they were spending their marketing budget on and strategically chose when to reflect the new context in which they operate.

Let the world know you are still viable, and remind them of what you can and are doing for them. Promote new programs or services that you will be rolling out shortly to maintain interest and build anticipation that better times are on the horizon. It shows commitment, strength, and confidence, and it will attract new customers. One example from the article was Reckitt Benckiser, the maker of household goods such as Dettol, Lysol, Durex, Air Wick, Clearasil, Scholl, and Finish.

In the recession following the 2008 financial crash, the company launched a marketing campaign aimed at persuading its consumers to continue purchasing its more expensive and better performing brands, despite the harsh economic climate. Increasing its advertising outlays by 25% in the face of reduced marketing by competitors, Reckitt Benckiser actually grew revenues by 8% and profits by 14%, when most of its rivals were reporting profit declines of 10% or more. They viewed advertising as an investment rather than an expense.

Reckitt Benckiser did not take the typical knee-jerk reaction to the financial meltdown. They evaluated the situation and took action. They determined that people still need their product and successfully invested in their more expensive brands.

Once again, act, not react.

Stepping Stones for Business Success

1. **Act Don't React.**

2. **Be prepared to press the reset button.**

3. **You don't know how strong you are until strong is your only option.**

CHAPTER 16

Ask For What You Need

The real thrill of business and life is the process, the quality of interactions and relationships, and the value you contribute to others.

Jay Abraham

S ure, you worked hard, but let's face it, without the right alliances, where would you be? No one makes it entirely on their own. The most successful people all point to a list of individuals who were there for them with guidance, encouragement, knowledge, experience, and connections. The most successful people know that what you don't know can hurt you.

STRATEGIC ALLIANCES AND RELATIONAL CAPITAL

Are you honest enough to admit to yourself that you don't know what you don't know?

As stated earlier in this book and it is worth repeating here . . . there are many reasons why businesses struggle or fail, but one reason most people don't acknowledge is this: Too many business owners don't know what they don't know, and they are either not willing or able to bring in the necessary expertise. And what I hear most often is: "We are smart, and we'll figure it out," or worse, they bring in the wrong people. Even the best and worst doctors need specialists just as the best and worst businesses need specialists, too.

It is not just about what you know that will determine success or failure; it's also about what you don't know. And sometimes, what you know is not nearly as important as who you know. THE TAG TEAM is an organization you should know. THE TAG TEAM is a partnership of experts in business from Organizational Development to Finance, from marketing to scaling.

Between my company, "Life Altering Events" and "The Abraham Group" – headed by Jay Abraham, arguably the best marketing mind and business builder in the world, we have been where you are now and know how to get you to where you want to go. Jay Abraham alone has increased the bottom lines of more than 10,000 clients by over $21B.

Why do you need to know THE TAG TEAM? THE TAG TEAM members have a vested interest in seeing the next generation of businesses thrive.

We partner with startup founders and organizations looking to scale. We bring in the necessary strategic partners and relational capital on an as-needed basis.

This is an "Elite and Exclusive program for entrepreneurs who are looking to make a major impact." As I said in the beginning, Great achievements come from great adversity. There are so many opportunities during this time of adversity if you know where to look and how to structure the process.

> *You will find that in order to be successful, you have to first want to make other people successful...*
>
> *When you make everyone else's life better, your life automatically opens up and expands monstrously.*
>
> Jay Abraham

Now how do we find the rocks so we can walk on water? When a company or organization approaches us, we look at five things BEFORE including them in the family.

1. How did you get to where you are? The answer we hear most often is we bootstrapped up to this point. Bootstrapping is great if you ever get on Oprah, but it says to me you have no money

and are most likely wasting your time. The first question is do you have enough money, and do you know the right people who can guide you through the swamp.

2. We examine your strategy to understand WHY you want to start or expand or, now since COVID-19, change your business. What value does it provide? WHY is far more important than WHAT you are doing! We will create or adjust your strategy so that your vision makes a deep connection with your customers. Value is the optimum word. Back in Chapter 14, we discussed the connection that value-driven companies like Harley Davidson and Apple have with their customers. Their customers are more like family. There is no other option. They will pay more and wait longer. Getting another product quicker or for a lower price is sacrilege.

   Apple, Harley Davidson, Southwest airlines inspire fierce loyalty with their buyers. Loyalty, real emotional value, exists in the brain of the buyer, not the seller.

   Simon Sinek- *Start With Why*

3. We create a business plan, including the key strategic partners, that corresponds with your strategy. As smart as you are, no one is good at everything. Our program will surround you with experts in areas you may not have or don't enjoy doing. We don't hire these experts; we bring them in on an as-needed basis. When the project is done, they go away. This is so important since what sinks many organizations is hiring the WRONG people. It may be a college professor or a frat brother, or a family member. They may be wonderful people, but the odds are they lack the level of expertise needed. Research shows that many of our 1st set of employees don't last. The job is too big or complex, or they or you get frustrated, and they leave. This exercise will cost you time you don't have and waste money you will never get back.

4. We build a branding/marketing/positioning program that differentiates you from the herd. Have you seen commercials for insurance companies? Of course, you have them run every couple of minutes. Some are catchy, most are obnoxious, but what is the message? It is we cost less than the other guy. To me, insurance companies are positioning themselves as a commodity. When you compete on price, it is a race to the bottom. You may be the low-cost option this month, but not next month. Maybe this is why people are always SHOPPING for insurance. To me, the lone exception is USAA. Their message focuses on serving the needs of two fiercely loyal groups, veterans and the military. Have you ever heard of an Apple, Harley Davidson, Tiffany, or Louis Vuitton commercial that focuses on price? They focus on value and exclusivity. They are the "club" that everyone aspires to join.

> We take price out of the equation. We develop fresh content that we push out on a consistent basis to your targeted customers. How many times do you see and hear the same old tired ads on the radio or TV? More times than not, you tune it out, or you can't figure out what product or service they are promoting. Repeating the same message over and over is a dated model. We bring in new energy and a series of messages that resonate. A real connection is made when customers hear what they want to hear, not what you want to say.

5. We examine how you have been funded so far and what you believe you need to LAUNCH your company. Let me repeat that – launch your company not go from point A to point B but from point A to point Z. I usually get the deer in the headlights look when I ask that question. Let me give you an example. I recently meet an organization that is developing an innovative process in the energy field. When we asked how much money they needed, the response was $600K. What are you going to do in 4 months when you run out of money? Their answer we will

go out for another round of funding. If you have ever gone out for funding, it is a major pain in the ass. You go into pitch deck hell; you give up more equity, lose time you will never get back, and fall further and further behind schedule. We suggested they ask for $10M. The response, we don't want to give up 30% or 40% of our business. Now think about this. Right now, they have 100% of nothing. With the proper funding and development, this could be a $150M company within five years. Isn't 60% of $150M worth more than 100% of nothing? Ask for what you really need. You are not going to scare away an investor by asking for a big number. In fact, it will improve your credibility because you have a realistic plan.

We have investor groups that will provide Relational Capital. First, we justify your assumptions. Determine how much money you need to launch when you need it, how the money will be used and when do you expect to be profitable. No investor is going to give you the $10M upfront. They will release the funds as milestones are achieved, AND they will provide the strategic partners to make sure you stay on task. Relational capital investors become your confidant. They have both a vested interest and are fully committed to helping you succeed.

Relational capital removes the constant going back and begging for funds. Yet, so many organizations continue to follow the high failure rate model from Chapter 4. They look for Angel investors, who are wonderful people but do not invest multiple millions of dollars. The organization will quickly run out of the initial funding and then finds itself in pitch deck hell over and over, looking for more money. The investor world is fairly small. When they see a pattern of an organization constantly returning for more funding, the relational capital investors walk away.

Why does this plan work? Because what you don't know can hurt you, and who you know can help you navigate the swamp.

Let me leave you with this: None of us is in this alone. The secret to walking on water is to know where the rocks are. Contact me. We know where the rocks are, and so will you. Let's face it, our professional life is important, but so is our personal life. When you don't know where the rocks are, both will sink. In the next chapter, I will discuss that life has to be more than just making a living.

Stepping Stones for Business Success

1. **Strategic Partners and Relational Capital matter**
2. **Think differently – How can the TAG TEAM help you?**
3. **Who can help you find the rocks?**

CHAPTER 17

Life Is More Than Just Making a Living

You know what is best for you and should follow it, rather than the promptings of others.

Gina Mazza – *Everything Matters, Nothing Matters*

How often have you found yourself so completely immersed in your business or your career that you become a spectator in the other areas of your life? Have you ever looked back on your life and wondered *if only...*? If only I had said this, taken that job, moved to that city, or spent more time with my family, how different would my life be now? Of course, you have!! Does it usually occur when you are sad or frustrated? We have all heard the statement by Lewis Carroll: "IN THE END... We only regret the chances we didn't take, the relationships we were afraid to have, and the decisions we waited too long to make."

Well, you are not alone. Everyone at times looks back with regret and wonders, "if only." I did at many low points in my life. The worst-case was after a very difficult divorce. While I was in the middle of my self-pity party, my best friend told me, "Frank, there is nothing new to see in the past. Besides, why are you looking behind you? You're not going that way." So, I picked up the pieces and started moving forward both personally and professionally. Some days I took one step forward. Other days four steps backward, but every day my goal was to keep moving forward.

2020 brought a great deal of unwanted change to the world. The COVID-19 crisis, unemployment, looming recession, shelter in place, quarantine, working from home, and homeschooling have forced us all to change. We all know the only constant in life is change, yet change is the one thing most people fear. Why? Because it is the fear of the unknown. People like stability, and change disrupts stability. It makes us ask questions like, "How is the change going to impact my life, my job, my income, my family?" It is frustrating and depressing. But I have met so many people who are using this time to re-evaluate, reflect, redirect and reinvent both their lives and their outlook on life.

Pre 2020, if you are like most people, there was never time to re-evaluate, reflect and redirect. We would get out of bed before sunrise and jump on the treadmill of life that constantly went faster and faster. By the end of the day, we went to bed too exhausted to get any real rest and got up a few hours later to start again. We weren't living; we were existing. I have been there. I felt every little thing mattered, then realized very little really matters.

Now amid all the chaos we are facing, I have been able to talk with a number of people who are using this time to look inwardly in the hope of finding a sense of calm, peace, and meaning. These people have asked me, "Do I even want to return to my old normal, my old job, my old habits, with all the stress and anxiety? I want to be alive with a capital A." There has to be a better way. Maybe this is the opportunity to change. But how do we change? What do we change? And the real question - Do we really want to change?

I recently read in the introduction of the book *Everything Matters, Nothing Matters* by my friend Gina Mazza, it stated:

> *In order for people to embrace and activate change, they have to feel it is both possible AND important.*

In order to determine if something is both possible and important, we have to look at the facts. What do I need to know or do to make the seemingly impossible possible? Are the facts important enough for me to take action?

Brene Brown wrote in her book *Dare to Lead*:

Why are facts and data important? Because in the absence of data, we will always make up false narratives to support a position.

The facts may say it is possible, but is it important enough to act. Changing our life or at least our outlook on life is hard because change is hard. Whenever we face anything hard, rationalizations and false narratives will come into play. It is just not the right time; how am I going to do this; I'll start when I get this project done. We fall into what my wife calls "dithering," which means focusing on or being distracted by other things, usually unimportant things which both wastes our time and drains our energy.

David Asprey called this "decision fatigue" in his book *Game Changers*

We all have a willpower muscle in the anterior cingulate cortex of our brain that starts each day full of energy. Every decision we make, be it trivial or important drains this energy. It is called decision fatigue, so focus your energy on decisions that will improve your life.

It is easier to cling to our status quo than take action that will lead to life altering decisions. For many people, something dramatic must occur before they take action on what is possible and important. Well, folks, 2020 may well be that tipping point. The old normal is gone, and it will likely never return. Now we are forced to become focused, to take a deep dive into who we are and what we want.

Aren't you worth loving what you do rather than just making a living? Don't you want to get up every morning excited to get started instead of dreading the drudgery of another day? Wouldn't working and living your passion make you feel alive with a capital A?

Passion and love are inextricably intertwined because they both arise from the heart. When you follow your passion, you will love your life.

Janet and Chris Attwood – *The Passion Test*

So, what is stopping you? Can you define your passion? Most people can't, which is why they aren't living their passion. Then there are people who know what their passion is but get stuck trying to figure how to make it happen. Once you commit and start on the path toward your passion, you will be amazed that doors will open. If you still are not sure about your passion, take the Passion Test found in Janet and Chris Attwood's book *The Passion Test*.

The "how" of living your passions is the result of being aligned with the flow of natural law with your "higher self" . . . The excitement is in the journey. The happiness that comes from achieving a goal is fleeting at best. Happiness arises spontaneously when you love the process.

Janet and Chris Attwood – *The Passion Test*

Sometimes we need a 2x4 between the eyes before we take action. The 2x4 can be many things, the loss of a job, divorce, death of a loved one, a job that brings you no joy, etc.

Deepak Chopra said:

Each person's tale involves some moment of trauma or questioning that leads them into a "shatter of the self" – which is what happens when "we don't know who we are." Deepak Chopra – from the book by – Gina Mazza – Everything Matters, Nothing Matters

For my friend Lauren Ward Larsen, it was a near-death experience during her pregnancy. She was hospitalized for several months, including multiple surgeries, blood transfusions, and dialysis sessions while her newborn daughter lived with her family. After her release from the hospital, there were many more months of rehabilitation. During this time, she and her husband made some hard decisions about what is really important in life.

As she wrote in her book *Zuzu's Petals*:

> *Twelve-hour workdays in corporations that have no vested interest in our happiness or creative expression were the first to fall by the wayside. We immediately eliminated phrases like "someday we'll..." from our vocabulary...And to fill the void of their departure, we increased our use of two words: Why not?*

Lauren Ward Larsen – *Zuzu's Petals*

Hopefully, it won't take a near-death experience for you to find your passion. Living your passion brings a sense of freedom to life. Your life will be different, and that can be frightening, but change often brings clarity to the chaos of life. She and her husband had a conversation about the definition of existentialism:

> *It's about the personal responsibility that comes with absolute freedom. In other words, don't wait around for the promise of great things in the afterlife.*
>
> *Get off your ass and create the life you want here and now.*

Lauren Ward Larsen – *Zuzu's Petals*

MAKE MEMORIES

Back in the introduction, I discussed the trauma I experienced with my daughters when my wife left. I left a very high-paying job and high-level position in high-tech, moved to another state, put my daughters into new schools, and took over an insurance agency. One thing about insurance is you make very little money in the first few years. I was angry. Angry at my wife. Angry at the circumstance. Angry at the world. One Saturday, I received a call from the former owner of the agency. He asked me how things were going. My anger and sarcasm got the better of me, and I snapped. "Thirty days ago, I was running a fifty-million-dollar company with over 100 people who would jump up to help if I just lifted my head. Today I am cleaning toilets in your old office. How do you think things are going?"

While I fell off a cliff financially, I gained time time to be available as a full-time Dad. During one of my Roku TV interviews with my friend Sara Westbrook, we talked about some of the trade-offs people make in life. One of the trade-offs is the exchange of money and time. As you make more money, your logical brain says we need more. If I am happy making $100,000, making $200,000 will double my happiness. You will have more money and even less time. Then Sara said she read an article about the science of happiness. People were given a number of options to gauge happiness; more time, more money, more power, etc. Per Sara, the number one factor for happiness is more time. This makes sense. The old death bed story is, no one wishes they had spent more time working.

This made me think about my early post-divorce time. I recall a friend telling me, "Make damn sure you attend all of your children's events. They won't remember all the ones you made, but they will remember every one you missed." He then told me when his son was younger; he missed several events. One time his son was flying back to town from a soccer tournament. "I knew his mother, and I could not be there to pick him up or be there when he arrived home, so I sent a limo, thinking it would be a big thrill." His son's teammates were are jealous. "Wow – you get to ride in a limo." His son, however, was not so thrilled. He had no one with whom to share his adventure except the limo driver. When he arrived home, there was no one to greet him and no one called. He just went to his room and played video games.

My friend then said something that cut right to my heart. "Frank, you know the song *Cat's in the Cradle* by Harry Chapin. The one where the son is always asking the Dad to do something with him, but the Dad is too busy, and the son would say, 'I'm gonna be like you, dad, you know I'm gonna be like you.' Then the Dad retires and calls the son, who is now too busy. The song ends with the Dad saying, 'And as I hung up the phone, it occurred to me he'd grown up just like me. My boy was just like me.' Well, Frank, that is my story. Don't let it become yours." This nearly brought me to tears. I was so unhappy because I was making far less money until I realized I could be making memories with my daughters.

My daughters and I had time. We went to the ocean, to Disney on Ice, to professional sporting events, movies, plays, shopping trips to San Francisco, to a week in Rome, Italy, to Marine World, to their dance recitals, softball and volleyball tournaments, etc. My daughters are now adults, and when we get together, they always talk about all the fun we had doing all these adventures. We look at the pictures together, smile, and revel in telling the stories. They don't speak fondly about the month I spent in Brazil or other times I was away. When Sara, heard this she told me, "Frank, you exchanged money and power for memories. You can lose your job, your money, your big house, and God forbid your health, but memories, memories are forever." The last thing Sara said during our interview was, "Frank, we can stop chasing perfection because it doesn't exist. However, we are fully capable of reflection and redirection of our thoughts, choices, and deeds."

I re-married after my daughters were out of the house and starting their own lives. Now when my new wife and I look at our children and grandchildren, I know the choice to make memories and now working to help people and organizations thrive personally and professionally was the right choice.

So, are you still struggling personally or professionally? Are you unhappy with the direction or lack of direction in your life? If the obstacles life dumps on you seem overwhelming, please do these three things:

1. Look up
2. Get up
3. Never ever give up

So now you know that **the secret** to Walking on Water is to know where the rocks are! You are not in this alone. Contact me. My team and I will help.

Stepping Stones for Business Success

1. **Make memories**
2. **Perfection doesn't exist; however, we are fully capable of reflection and redirection of our thoughts, choices, and deeds.**
3. **Get off your ass and create the life you want here and now.**

CHAPTER 18

Personal Life Landmines

I am not a product of my circumstances. I am a product of my decisions.

Stephen Covey

After spending years and thousands of dollars with counselors, I finally started to come to grips with the challenges of my youth and the military. While these experiences shaped much of how I thought and acted, I still had control over my decisions. Unfortunately, those decisions involving relationships were not good. I was the oldest of five children born within eight years. My role was to be the protector and defender of my siblings. Any time someone picked on them, I would aggressively confront the other person(s). Many times, it turned into a physical altercation. (Back then, fights did not include guns or knives). Win or lose, the message was clear, do not mess with my family.

My youngest sister tells a story about when she was in sixth or seventh grade, that one time I was umpiring the bases at a local baseball game. She was sitting on the bleachers down the right-field line when a young man came over and sat next to her. Between innings, I glanced over, and not recognizing the guy, I walked toward them to get a better look. At the end of the next inning, I looked back, and the young man was gone. After the game, my sister was not pleased and told me, "I like that guy, and when you gave him that look, that glare you have, he asked, 'Is that your brother Frank?' I said yes, and then he said, 'Let him know I was just talking,' and he left. You scare people away just by looking at them."

One counselor told me this protector model is often called the White Knight Syndrome.

I asked her to explain. She said, "White knight syndrome is a term used to describe someone who feels compelled to 'rescue' people in intimate relationships, often at the expense of their own needs. You feel compelled to rush to save the perceived damsel in distress." Then she said, "You keep repeating the same process. You are attracted and drawn to the same type of woman. You are actively drawn to women who seem helpless and in need of support (such as those with a history of untreated trauma or self-harm) and treat them as extensions of yourself, criticizing and controlling them under the guise of 'just trying to help.' Now at first, they may have needed and/or welcomed your actions, but eventually, they or you outgrew the situation, and the relationship failed. In short, Frank, **your picker is broken.**" Oh my god, this is the classic definition of insanity... "Doing the same thing and expecting a different result."

As I left the session, I went back through my relationship history. From high school to the military to college, to pre-marriage, to marriages, to post-divorce relationships, and she was right. I kept repeating the same toxic situations. In doing research for this book, I found an article in www.bigthink.com by Robby Berman from May 17, 2016, titled: "Why am I repeating the same mistakes?"

> It has to do with neural pathways that get created as we do things. When we do something right, a neural pathway is created. Unfortunately, a pathway is also created when we something wrong... So, the reason we keep making the same mistakes is that we slip by default back into existing neural pathways.

OK, so it has to do with the wiring, that my choices have developed in my brain and not solely that I am a "dumbass." Think about it. How often do we see people continuously drawn to the same situation or same type of personality such as:

- The bad boy
- The party girl
- Someone like their mother or father
- An alcoholic or other type of addict
- An abuser, mentally, physically, emotionally
- Someone in the same line of business (this is very pervasive in the military)

Why? It is not simply because it is something we know or something we perceive that makes us comfortable. It is also from the neural pathways we have built over the years. Does this mean we will never break this toxic and destructive cycle? No! Our brains can re-learn, be re-wired, so to speak. How? Once you know what you want to work on, consider these points. Alice Boyes Ph.D. writes in *Psychology Today*, September 21, 2018

1. **Vowing to never make a particular mistake again is the wrong approach.** You will make the same mistake again. However, you can change your focus to developing practical strategies that will help you make less severe mistakes less often.

2. **Develop strategies for prevention.** You need to take a problem-solving approach that's tailored to your exact circumstances, one that's actually doable rather than aspirational. Your strategies should feel like a reflection of yourself and be things you'll want to do, rather than seeming unappealing.

3. **Put aside time and mental energy.** The reality of life is that we don't always have the time or mental space available to mindfully address self-sabotaging habits. That's normal, but until you have that energy available, you probably won't do anything to turn around your patterns. What times during your day/week do you have enough cognitive energy available for self-strategizing?

4. **Develop strategies for harm minimization**. Harm minimization is about having a safety net—a therapist, a very trusted friend, a sponsor, etc.

5. **Understand your "Seemingly Irrelevant Decisions."** Seemingly Irrelevant Decisions are decisions that set you down the path towards a self-regulation failure. It is a form of self-sabotage.

So, what role does culture plays in the behavior patterns of men and women? Keep reading.

Stepping Stones for Business Success

1. **We are the result of our decisions, not our environment**
2. **White Knight Syndrome isn't helping anyone**
3. **Neural Pathways can be reprogrammed**
4. **Seemingly irrelevant decision leads to self-regulated failure**

CHAPTER 19

How Did We Get Here

I have great respect for the past. If you don't know where you've come from, you don't know where you're going.

Maya Angelou

When my Life Altering Events show was on the radio, I was asked if I would be interested in doing an episode regarding a man's perspective on relationships; I was intrigued. Let's face it; this topic doesn't get much press or exposure mainly because men don't openly talk about their emotions, fears, or insecurities regarding relationships. I decided to take a look back at the culturalization of men. There was a great deal of feedback back pro and con. I decided to put it in this book and include research I discovered regarding the culturalization of women. I am looking for your reaction(s).

Believe it or not, ladies, the vast majority of men want a deep and meaningful relationship. They want someone to share their life, hopes, dreams, and, yes, fears. One major problem is we don't know how. Much of the culturalization of males going back to the cavemen days is hiding your emotions, showing any vulnerability, fixing things yourself – even when all your partner wants is for you to listen, not fix the problem.

Many males feel they are being attacked when their partner attempts to delve into emotional conversations, particularly if the conversations include the words "Why don't you?" or "You never!" The stereotypical male reaction is to withdraw or become angry, and both are relationship poison. I am told women will process the actions and reactions of men both internally and with friends, while men tend to withdraw more or ignore potential warning signs adding more poison.

So, I went back through my notes for talks and workshops I have attended or presented regarding the culturalization of males.

The term that kept coming up is Toxic Masculinity! If you haven't heard this term, you will. It has become a trendy topic on social media, blogs, and talk shows. The first time I heard it, I thought it was a new disease that had been discovered.

WHAT IS TOXIC MASCULINITY

Let's look at the term, Toxic Masculinity. Webster defines it as:

Those aspects of traditional masculinity perceived to reinforce aggression, emotionlessness, and other negative qualities, theorized as a component of masculine ideology, particularly in the United States.

It is often validated by the statement "boys will be boys."

The concept of toxic masculinity is used in psychology and gender studies to refer to certain norms of masculine behavior in North America and Europe associated with harm to society, women, and men themselves.

Psychiatrist Frank Pittman wrote about the ways in which men are harmed by traditional masculine norms, suggesting this includes shorter lifespans, greater incidence of violent death, and ailments such as lung cancer and cirrhosis of the liver and suicide.

Hmmm, it sounds like a cultural thing that has been reinforced since the cavemen's days. The strongest individual became the leader based on the need to survive. Given that men are generally physically stronger than women, the alpha male became the undisputed and unchallenged leader. It seemed to make sense back then, but I haven't seen much of a need in the last 300 plus years to hunt down a water buffalo with sticks and rocks to fend off a saber-toothed tiger. Yet this pattern of defining and raising boys continues and still occurs today.

Toxic masculinity is thus defined by adherence to traditional male gender roles that restrict the kinds of emotions allowable for boys and men to express, including social expectations that men seek to be dominant (the "alpha male") and limit their emotional range primarily to expressions of anger.

This concept of toxic masculinity is not intended to demonize men or male attributes but rather to emphasize the harmful effects of conformity to certain traditional masculine ideal behaviors such as dominance, self-reliance, and competition.

This is not an indictment on men. The vast majority of men understand there is a time and a place for competition and self-reliance. Think of the late Kobe Bryant. No one was more competitive or ferocious in his profession, but he successfully compartmentalized the various aspects of his life and became a beloved hero to both men and women. However, some are inclined to take these characteristics to the extreme. This is where problems occur.

Our goal is to get this topic out in the open for conversation and education. Open discourse in a positive and supportive environment is the key to understanding and altering the harmful effects of toxic masculinity.

Contemporary expectations of masculinity can produce such "toxic" effects as violence (including sexual assault and domestic violence), "sexual excess" (promiscuity), excessively risky and/or socially irresponsible behaviors including substance abuse, dysfunction in relationships, and suicide.

Vulnerability is seen as a sign of weakness—the weak must be weeded out. Too many men perform self-weeding when they feel vulnerable. In 2016 there were 45,000 suicides in the United States. 33,750—75 percent were men.

This type of behavior is both magnified and glorified daily. A great deal of money is paid to and for content directly or indirectly supporting toxic masculinity. Some examples include:

- Violence in video games - The game-winner inflicts the greatest amount of violence and mayhem.

- Violence in movies - Graphic and often unnecessary acts of violence.
- Athletics - Athletics, and competition at their core are healthy and positive. From early youth sports to professional leagues, competition builds character, teamwork, etc. For those few who are blessed with the physical attributes and skills, athletics provide an extremely lucrative lifestyle that is often envied by men prone to toxic masculinity behavior.

The dark side of athletics includes: breaking the rules in order to win at all costs, a sense of entitlement and privilege (rules don't apply to you), locker room behavior that demeans women, and others who were not blessed with the skills or talent.

- TV shows (such as Mad Men) - Programs that depict a time when overt harassment, infidelity, and demeaning of women and subordinates, excessive drinking (three cocktail lunches) was accepted and rewarded.
- Abusive and overbearing bosses and managers - People who are risen to positions of power, wealth, and prominence who use their power to suppress, harass, and abuse people.
- Speeches and actions of political leaders - Openly mocking, demeaning, inciting, or suggesting acts of violence or harassment.

So, what do we do? As men, we have to realize, understand and accept that boorish and abusive behavior in any form to any person is not acceptable. We cannot continue to condone or look the other way when we find ourselves in an environment where toxic behavior is occurring.

Why are so many men confused about what to do?

The #METoo movement scared the hell out of most men. The statement I heard most often is, "Now what are we supposed to do or not do?" Many of us were taught growing up that boys and men are supposed to be strong. Strong meaning, we don't cry; we don't talk about emotions or feelings; we do whatever it takes to be successful; we are self-reliant enough to solve whatever issue or problems or situation that occurs. For those of us who are old enough to remember, the ideal American Man was the Marlboro Man (a rugged individual, out working alone, riding his horse, who didn't need anything or anyone).

Our image of American life was from the TV shows, like Donna Reed, Father Knows Best, and Ozzie & Harriett, where the father went to work and the mother stayed home, ran errands, cleaned the house wearing a dress, heels, and pearls. If women did work, they were secretaries who made coffee, answered phones, and filed papers; or they were teachers who were portrayed as glorified babysitters.

Then in the 1960s and 70s, more women started entering the workforce, often out of economic necessity. They were putting off marriage (less and less were getting married at 18 or 19). Women had more choices. More and more women graduated from college and were capable of supporting themselves. They didn't need a man to be the sole provider and protector. In many cases, they didn't need a man at all.

The women's movement started. Women were openly and aggressively speaking out; there were marches and rallies; women were starting businesses; being elected to public office. *According to Pew Research, January 15, 2021,*

> *In 2021, 144 of 539 seats in Congress – or 27% – are held by women. There are 120 women in the House (27%) and 24 in the Senate (24%). That represents a 50% increase from the 96 women who were serving in the 112th Congress a decade ago.*

According to *Fortune Magazine, on August 4, 2020,* 38 Fortune 500 companies are headed by women (5.6%).

Today, women outnumber men in college, grad schools, and STEM (science, technology, engineering, and math) programs.

The newer wave of TV sitcoms was coming out where the man is portrayed as a buffoon, and the woman is the strong leader of the family.

Man and husband bashing became more common on TV (Modern Family, The Big Bang Theory, Everyone Loves Raymond, Black-ish. etc...).

For some men, this was more than they could handle. The men's myth was shattered! Men discovered that we cannot do it on our own, whether we admitted it or not. We needed our spouse/significant other to work to make ends meet. We were vulnerable and had no training or support system to help us. Men have to unlearn a lifetime of training and culture.

Some men became resentful. This paradigm shift preyed on their male insecurity, "We no longer the king of our castle. We have to remain in control and put these women in their place. We want things the way they use to be."

Well, guys, those days are gone. They are not coming back. A new order is emerging where men and women will work and live together in a collaborative and mutually beneficial manner. It is going to take time and patience. But it is going to happen.

THE "CULT OF DOMESTICITY"

The late author, Dorothy W. Hartman, wrote an article, *Lives of Women*, in *Connor Prairie*. It is one of the most comprehensive historical views of the lives, expectations, and evolution of women. In the article, Ms. Hartman referred to the Cult of Domesticity. So, what is this cult?

According to Wikipedia:

> *The cult of domesticity, also known as the cult of true womanhood, is an opinion about women in the 1800s. They believed that women should stay at home and should not do any work outside of the home.*

There were four things they believed that women should be:

1. More religious than men (piety)
2. Pure in heart, mind, and body (purity)

3. Submissive to their husbands (submissiveness)

4. Staying at home (domesticity)

This ideology would strongly discourage women from obtaining an education. This ideology was thought to elevate the moral status of women and be beneficial for them in ways such as living lives of higher material comfort. It made the roles of wife and being a mother more important in society.

It was this type of thinking that led to the mindset "Keep women barefoot and pregnant."

When the United States became a country, it espoused Life, Liberty, and the Pursuit of Happiness. Yet, women were considered chattel (property) and were not given their right to vote. A wife's earnings were her husband's property and not her own. In 1925, wives were considered to be a man's property.

Per the article the *Lives of Women*, other accepted practices marginalizing women included:

1. A married woman could not enter into binding contracts except for "necessities" and could not enter into executory contracts (i.e., contracts to be performed in the future).

2. There was no criminal liability for offenses other than murder committed by a husband against a wife or vice versa (e.g., rape and domestic violence of a husband directed at a wife were legal).

3. A husband had a right to physically discipline his wife or hire a third-party, public official to do so on his behalf. Adultery was a crime, and wives were generally the ones most likely to be prosecuted for it.

4. A wife was legally obligated to maintain her domicile with her husband and could be legally compelled (with third-party assistance if necessary) to return to it.

5. There was no civil liability between spouses who were one person under the law (i.e., spouses could not sue each other in court).

6. Wives could not (and still cannot in most circumstances) testify against their husbands in court on any matter.

7. A wife's lawsuit against a third person would generally be brought by the husband either on her behalf or in cases such as personal injury suits for "loss of consortium."

8. Wives generally had no right to inherit from their own families.

9. Women, in general, could not vote or run for public office or serve on juries, or be drafted to serve in the military.

10. Children born during the marriage were conclusively presumed to be a husband's children even if this was highly implausible as a matter of fact, and children born outside of marriage were illegitimate and had no legal rights at all vis-a-vis their fathers.

Advancements by and for women have always met with resistance. Things we now take for granted, such as the right to vote, to own property, to have a credit card, did not occur until there were protests and finally legislation. Here are some examples:

1920 – 19th Amendment prohibits denying the right to vote on the basis of sex	1921 – Equal Rights Amendment originally introduced to Congress. Still not ratified.	1942-1944 – Women take "nontraditional work" during WWII (e.g., Rosie the Riveter)	1946-1964– Baby Boom. A Force Awakens. Awareness of effects of demographic shifts
1960 – FDA approves a birth control pill. Rx limited in 1961 to married women.	1963 – Equal Pay Act (EPA)	1964 – Civil Rights Act	1967 – Age Discrimination in Employment Act (ADEA)

1972 – Title IX of the Education Amendments Act	1974 - The Equal Credit Opportunity Act allowing women to own property and credit cards.	1991 – Civil Rights Act adds compensatory and punitive damages in civil rights violations	2017 – #MeToo. Adding the hashtag and celebrities fuels the movement, which begun in 2006.
2006 - "Me Too" 2017 - "Me Too" gained National attention	2021 – 38 women CEOs, Fortune 500	2021 – 144 Women in Congress 24 in Senate – 24% 120 in House - 27% Woman Vice President	"We're an equal opportunity employer. All applicants will be considered for employment without attention to race, color, religion, sex, sexual orientation, gender identity, national origin, veteran or disability status."

The United States was a country for 144 years before the 19th Amendment was passed. The 19th Amendment to the U.S. Constitution granted American women the right to vote, a right known as women's suffrage, and was ratified on August 18, 1920, ending almost a century of protest. While the right to vote was now law, there were states that tried to suppress women from voting.

Prior to the Equal Credit Opportunity Act of 1974, 198 years after becoming a nation, banks and other financial institutions denied married women in the U.S. credit cards or loans in their own name. Single women also had trouble getting credit. The Equal Credit Opportunity Act of 1974 "prohibits discrimination on the basis of race, color, religion, national origin, sex, marital status, or age in credit transactions." The law was passed mainly through the efforts of the late Ruth Bader Ginsberg.

The Equal Rights Amendment (ERA) has still not been added to the Constitution. It was introduced in 1923. The ERA states, "Equality of rights under the law shall not be denied or abridged by the United States or by any State on account of sex. The Congress shall have the power to enforce, by appropriate legislation, the provisions of this article." On January 15, 2020, Virginia became the 38th state to ratify the ERA. As of January 6, 2021, the ERA has still not been added to the Constitution.

Actress Amy Poehler wrote; It takes years as a woman to unlearn what you have been taught to be sorry about. In spite of the legislation, women still face oppression. For example:

- *Inc. Magazine* Aug 2019 reported women are paid 85% for similar positions and work. Women make less than a man for comparable job title and duties
- Women pay more for simple things like dry cleaning
- Women remain the primary caregiver
- In the COVID world, more women are leaving the workforce due to demands of shelter at home, lack of adequate child care, and distant learning for children.
- While sexual harassment has been illegal for years, it was largely swept under the rug and rarely enforced until the full tsunami of the #METoo movement in 2017.
- In a 2019 interview with ABC's Cheri Preston, research shows there are more Fortune 500 CEOs named John than all women CEOs combined.
- In the same interview with Cheri Preston, there are 12.3 million women-owned businesses that generate $2 Trillion annually, and 67% of the wealth is controlled by women. Yet, most of these successful owners are not taken seriously. For example – they are just augmenting their household income; they aren't included in the "good old boy networking activities and funders who think it is a hobby."

Planned Parenthood published a report called What are gender roles and stereotypes? The stereotypes for young girls and women were of particular interest.

Gender roles for girls and women are generally expected to dress in typically feminine ways and be polite, accommodating, and nurturing.

The article defined four basic kinds of gender stereotypes for women:

1. Personality traits — For example, women are often expected to be accommodating and emotional, while men are usually expected to be self-confident and aggressive.
2. Domestic behaviors — For example, some people expect that women will take care of the children, cook, and clean the home, while men take care of finances, work on the car, and do the home repairs.
3. Occupations — Some people are quick to assume that teachers and nurses are women and that pilots, doctors, and engineers are men.
4. Physical appearance — For example, women are expected to be thin and graceful, while men are expected to be tall and muscular. Men and women are also expected to dress and groom in ways that are stereotypical to their gender (men wearing pants and short hairstyles, women wearing dresses and make-up.

Hyperfemininity is the exaggeration of stereotyped behavior that's believed to be feminine. Hyperfeminine folks exaggerate the qualities they believe to be feminine. This may include being passive, naive, sexually inexperienced, soft, flirtatious, graceful, nurturing, and accepting. In 2021, women who push against these stereotypes have been referred to as "Militant Feminist.

Give the differences in the culturation of men and women over centuries; it is not hard to see why finding and sustaining a strong, lasting, loving relationship can be such a challenge.

How can we avoid gender stereotypes?

Planned Parenthood suggests the following: You probably see gender stereotypes all around you. You might also have seen or experienced sexism or discrimination based on gender. There are ways to challenge these stereotypes to help everyone — no matter their gender or gender identity — feel equal and valued as people.

1. Point it out — Magazines, TV, film, and the Internet are full of negative gender stereotypes. Sometimes these stereotypes are hard for people to see unless they're pointed out. Be that person! Talk with friends and family members about the stereotypes you see and help others understand how sexism and gender stereotypes can be hurtful.

2. Be a living example — Be a role model for your friends and family. Respect people regardless of their gender identity. Create a safe space for people to express themselves and their true qualities regardless of society's gender stereotypes and expectations.

3. Speak up — If someone is making sexist jokes and comments, whether online or in person, challenge them.

4. Give it a try — If you want to do something that's not normally associated with your gender, think about whether you'll be safe doing it. If you think you will give it a try. People will learn from your example.

Now that we know where we have been let's see how we can avoid the landmines we all face today.

Stepping Stones for Business Success

1. The impact of culturalization on males – Toxic masculinity
2. The impact of culturalization on females – Cult of Domesticity
3. Legislation to level the playing field
4. Gender roles and stereotypes

CHAPTER 20

Leave Work at Work

"The pursuit of 'balance' implies that work and life are two separate spheres competing for our attention in a zero-sum game. I prefer to see them as a continuum, flowing into and influencing one another."

Roger Ferguson

For those of us who invested in our education, are or were strapped with student loans, and doing our best to not only survive but thrive in our business career, leaving work at work is challenging. Every organization talks about supporting a work/life balance. Some even put that statement in their annual report and recruiting material. It is the right thing to say, but it is not reality. Corporate America will take every second of every minute of your life if you allow it to happen. No one I know started their career wanting to put in twelve-to-sixteen-hour days, or be on the road every week or finally going home only to spend more time on zoom or answering emails or working on your laptop. Yet, it happens far too often.

The job taking over your life creeps up on you. It starts with trying to meet short deadlines, then major projects, then managing a team, then more travel. Before you know it, you are sabotaging your relationship and family in the name of providing for your family. It makes no sense, right? It is almost like an addiction that you think you are controlling, but it is controlling and destroying you.

An example of this destructive pattern is described in my book *When the Wife Cheats*. The background is a young, rising corporate star selected to create a new division from scratch. He is focused and driven to make this division a major success. He is married with one young child.

We finally came upon a major request for a proposal from the Department of Corrections that we actually had a chance to win. It would be a multimillion-dollar deal, and the response was going to take over a year to prepare. I put together a team that consisted of a large defense contractor to act as prime contractor. This software house had the basic requirements and could modify the software, a project manager with strong connections and experience in corrections, and a lobbyist to help us work the political angle. Given that my staff was so inexperienced, I had them collect and compile the information I needed. I became the lead on the project, with my assistant handling all the administrative functions. Our defense contractor was based in San Diego, so I was spending a great deal of time there during the week and at home on weekends. Sometimes my wife and daughter would fly down on Friday, and we'd stay the weekend in San Diego. My daughter was about three and loved staying at the Embassy Suites. We would go down and look at the fish every day. She was mesmerized. We did all the touristy things in San Diego.

My wife started to get frustrated and depressed about my time away. We had a bout with post-partum depression after our daughter was born. Several of her family members, including her mother and sister, suffered from anxiety and depression. Her demeanor would frequently change from happy to sad or calm to angry. She would start to cry and tell me she couldn't deal with being a parent or with my traveling; she felt like a single parent. I had never experienced this and tried to be helpful, but with all my traveling, I know I wasn't giving her what she wanted.

She felt trapped at home with a baby and a husband on the road. I tried to be understanding, but this new division needed a major win, and my staff was basically worthless. My explanation didn't seem to help. One weekend there was a church picnic that my wife wanted us to attend. I was working on a major revision to a pricing spreadsheet at home and talking with my counterpart in San Diego. When it was time to leave for the picnic, I told my wife to go ahead, and I would come in an hour or so. The spreadsheet became overwhelming, and, of course, we had issues with the old-style PC. My one hour turned into three. By the time I made it to the picnic, everyone was packing up to leave. My wife was livid. She said, "This is another example of you not valuing me or what I want to do. I told you about this picnic three weeks ago and told you it was important. You promised to show up, and here you are at the end. I am sick of this."

I apologized again, but she would not hear it. I left for San Diego the next morning. I called her when I arrived and every day that week. For two days, she wouldn't even answer the phone. When she did, all she said is, "We're fine," and hung up.

Things didn't improve. My wife stayed very cold and distant. There was no intimacy between us. I understood why she was so angry, but we only had one stream of income, and the bills had to get paid, and the baby fed and clothed. The bid response, coupled with my wife's anger and depression were sucking the life out of me. She complained that even when I was home, "Your mind is on your goddamn project."

It doesn't take a rocket scientist to see where this relationship was headed. The wife found someone who would listen and give her support and comfort. It started as a one-time cry for help and evolved into a relationship that ended the marriage. I have been there too many times in my failed relationships and marriages.

So, how can you reduce the potential for your relationship to fail because you can't leave work at work? I am not a Ph.D. or counselor, or licensed therapist, so I can't give you therapeutic or clinical data. What I can offer are suggestions that may help.

1. Stop thinking you have to be involved in every aspect and every work decision. Yes, you are ultimately responsible, but that doesn't mean you have to do everything.

2. Micromanagers are anything but helpful, suffocating "creativity, productivity, and morale." Stop checking so often. You may think you're being helpful, but no one else does. Trust your team's abilities... Delegate until it bleeds. You will be surprised how people rise to the challenge. - *Richard Moran*

3. Create an environment of trust at work. Your ability to build trusting, human connections with the people who report directly to you will determine the quality of everything that follows. – *Kim Scott – Radical Candor*. It will also give us control freaks, the peace of mind that the world won't come to an end without us and we can spend time, quality time with our family.

4. Make a schedule and stick to it. I go in at this time, work like hell until that time, and then I go home.

5. Build in time to unwind. Do something that helps you to relax and decompress. It can be anything. Listen to music on the drive home – or in the COVID world before you walk out of your makeshift home office. Work out immediately before or after work. I use to go to an aerobics class at 5:30 in the morning before work and run 20 to 30 minutes on a treadmill immediately after work; in the COVID world, I put a "Total Gym" and treadmill in my house.

It cleared my head, helped me stay healthy, and allowed me to be more present at home.

6. Spend five to ten minutes as soon as you walk in the house just to ask your spouse and/or children, "Tell me what made you happy today." It can become a ritual everyone looks forward to. As your children grow and have after-school events, make it a weekly ritual. Your children will roll their eyes as they become "tweens," but it will become a fond memory.

7. Create a daily gratitude journal. If you don't like to write things down, then spend 5 minutes before you get out of bed or before you go to sleep to reflect on the things that make you and your family happy.

8. If your job requires you to travel, make sure you call, zoom, or face time daily with your spouse and children. Talk about their day, how much you miss and love them.

9. Put on the calendar a "Get Re-Acquainted" night with your significant other. This was one of my major failures. I always found time for my daughters but did not make the same effort for my wife.

10. Don't assume your loved ones understand being the "workaholic" is for them. They won't understand. All they see is their time isn't important enough for you.

I hope you don't discover, as I did, that no job or title or income or fame is worth clawing your way to the top, and then once you arrive, there is no one who matters standing with you. Believe me; professional success is not worth the price of a shattered life.

Let me end this chapter with this:

Professor Stewart Friedman of the Wharton School teaches leaders how to balance work and life because his research proved that leaders without balance make crappy leaders and crappy life partners.

What's next? Communication is the key. Keep reading

Stepping Stones for Business Success

1. **How the job taking over your life "creeps" up on you**
2. **Being present matters**
3. **Make time for family**
4. **Professional success is not worth the price of a shattered life**

CHAPTER 21

Dialogue Requires Deep Listening

We have two ears and one mouth so that we can listen twice as much as we speak.

Epictetus

A memorable line from the movie Cool Hand Luke is, "What we've got here is failure to communicate." How often do you hear "We don't talk anymore! You don't listen to me! Did you hear what I said?" Communication or lack of communication is a major relationship landmine. While I dislike stereotypes, I am going to use a few to make a point. For the most part, women are more open and willing to engage in long and detailed conversations with each other. We have all seen female friends spend several hours talking about an event that occurred and how they feel about it at lunch or on the phone or zoom. Then they can call the same person a few hours later or the next day and have another long conversation. Women see this as natural and normal and would like this to be the case with their relationship partner.

Men, on the other hand, tend not to talk nearly as much. Have you ever seen male friends together? Maybe they are watching a game? They can go several minutes without saying a word other than "nice catch" or "great pitch." There is not a great deal of deep or meaningful conversation. This is normal and natural for them, and they feel it should be the same way with their relationship partner.

Here is another example. When you call your parents' home, does your Dad's side of the conversation sound like this if you are a woman:

"Hi, how are you doing? Is everything OK? Is everyone healthy? How is work? How are the kids? Do you need anything? Ok, good, here is your mother." If you are a male, you may hear, "Did you see the game this week? Then, here is your mother." You have a much more complete and more engaging conversation with your mother, right?

Women tend to want details. Men are more interested in the cliff notes version of the story. Women want to know what and why a man is thinking about an issue. Men don't think that much, as many comedians have told us over the years. Women are better multi-taskers and can connect several different topics into one conversation. Men are more linear. Let's talk about one thing at a time. Let's come to a conclusion so I can go back to what I was doing. If these examples have some truth, then we have a built-in communication barrier that needs to be addressed, but how?

Earlier, I address this issue from a business perceptive; however, it is equally important for a healthy personal relationship. In the business world, communication and dialogue are considered soft skills. Let's review what we said about soft skills earlier in an earlier chapter. It is worth repeating here. Soft often implies easy. Well, news flash, folks, there is nothing soft or easy about effective communication. In fact, I have discovered soft skills are more difficult in personal than professional relationships. Why? No one's paycheck is directly involved. Let's go back to the conversation I had on soft skills with my good friend Gina Sharpe one morning over coffee in San Diego. As you recall, Gina has real estate operations in Phoenix and San Diego. She is one of the best listeners I know.

Here is a summary of our conversation:

Soft skills are non-technical skills that relate to how you work or engage in a relationship. They include how you interact with colleagues or loved ones, how you address or solve problems, and how you manage your words. Soft skills include:

- Communication skills – having a dialogue with someone, not talking at them

- Listening skills – listening to understand, not respond, not half-listening (male thing)
- Process time – allowing time to think then act, not react in crisis mode or anger
- Empathy – I am here for you

If we are having trouble developing soft skills professionally, this problem will carry over into our personal relationships. As we improve our soft skills in the workplace, in many cases, it doesn't carry over to our personal relationships.

Let me give you some examples
How many times has this occurred? The job pushed your stress level to maximum overload. Nothing went right. Your team cannot agree on a major issue, and the deadline is staring you in the face. So, you come home exhausted and just want to be left alone, have a drink or two, and try to unwind for a period of time? If your home life was like mine, you would walk into controlled chaos. Your spouse or partner is also exhausted and wants to vent about their situation. You are not interested in hearing more problems, so you either ignore your spouse or say something like, "Look, I dealt with complaints all damn day. I don't want to hear more." As soon as the words leave your mouth, you know this is not going to end well. Your spouse may say some type of expletive and remind you that you are not the only one in this relationship with a stressful job. You are both tired, frustrated, and now angry. So, what do you think comes next? The odds are you are not having a dialogue. You're aren't listening to understand; in fact, you're likely not listening at all. In the heat of the moment, you are not taking time to think before reacting, and empathy can't be found with two hands and a flashlight. I am willing to bet you both storm off to different areas of the house internally, justifying why your spouse is so inconsiderate. Now you are angry from work and home. If this scenario becomes the norm, both your personal and professional life is going to suffer. Like it or not, you

cannot separate one from the other. When one is not going well, the other will also be impacted.

The second example is like the first, but let's add children. Child A just had a snack, has to be taken to soccer practice, and child B needs to be picked up from band and needs to have something to eat. Both are going to need help with their math homework, which you didn't understand at their age, and your math skills haven't improved with time. Dinner for everyone still needs to occur, and you are trying to decide which fast-food place to use today. Your children are being children, and the tension and anxiety feel like an elephant is stepping on your chest. You and your spouse are rapidly approaching DEFCON 1. If this becomes the norm, your personal and professional life are going to crash and burn.

Now take scenario number 2, and let's throw COVID-19 into the equation. The entire family is at home 24x7. The children are doing remote learning using something called Zoom, which, if you are over 30, you have never heard of or never used and certainly don't know how to set up. Your house or apartment becomes a make-shift school and two offices (if you and your spouse are working). Your network carrier didn't expect COVID and does not have the necessary bandwidth for your entire city to be working from home. The network starts to freeze or just stop. Now, no one in the house is accomplishing anything productive, and if your network provider is like mine, your television isn't working either. You can't use a neighbor or friend's network because they are in the same predicament. You can't get into a store for food and supplies because panic buying is occurring, and stores have to limit the number of people entering. When you do get into the store, what you need to buy is sold out, and some clown is loading fifty packages of toilet paper into their minivan.

How are your soft skills working now?!

Let's go back to dialogue and connections. We discussed the importance in business, now how does it apply to personal life. Something I hear from people in a relationship is, "We have discussions all the time, but we aren't connecting." Many times, one person gets angry and shuts down, or it escalates into an all-out disagreement or intense argument. Therein lies the problem. Let's review discussion vs. dialogue one more time?

My good friend Nicole Bendaly, the President of K&Co in Toronto, writes in her book *Winner Instinct*:

> *Discussion, often called debate, tends to be an individual defining or defending his/her position or point of view. The goal is to win. In contrast, dialogue promotes shared understanding instead of individual understanding. In dialogue, no one is trying to win. The goal is to determine a solution to make a connection.*

My associate Susanna Bravo, MA, often tells me discussion is much like sympathy, and dialogue is like empathy. Again, what is the difference?

Sympathy creates distance

- "I am sorry for you"
- "Let me know if I can help."

Empathy brings closeness

- I am sorry, and I am here with you
- I am right here to go through it with you

Another way to look at this in a relationship is when one says, "let me know if I can help," but never offers (sympathy). And one shows up and engages without being asked (empathy).

So how do personal relationships find common ground for communication and connection? This is not one of my strengths. I will share what I have learned from trial and error, mainly error, and defer to experts. It is my understanding that while grand gestures (diamond earrings, elegant dinners, surprise him by wearing sexy lingerie, a romantic getaway) are one form of communication, they aren't the strongest ways to connect. OK, this blows a giant hole in what many men believe. A grand gesture is like a get-out-of-jail-free card for a few months or years with most men. I understand from several women counselors, grand gestures are nice, but the consistency of word and deed mean far more. Regardless of how big the grand gesture is, it counts as one thing.

Dr. Shannon Kolakowski, a Psychologist, and Author wrote a blog called The Single Best Thing You Can Do for Your Relationship. It appeared in the *HuffPost Contributor* platform 11/20/2012:

> *The deeper component has more to do with how you interact together rather than what you do together. It's called validation. Consistent, thoughtful validation of your partner's thoughts and feelings is the best thing you can do for your relationship... It is more important to feel heard, understood and listened to.*

I attended a play, the name escapes me, where a female bartender tells a guy having major problems in his relationship, "**The secret to a woman's heart is through her ears.** What you say and how you say it means more than grand gestures."

For men, listening and not offering a solution or a way to fix an issue is a foreign concept. Why are you telling me about this if you don't want something done? Men want to resolve the situation and move on. Women don't want men to fix the issue, they want to be heard and their feelings validated. Women want to share and have you listen to the details of what has occurred, tell you how it made them feel, and would like support or empathy. Again, not a strength for most men – particularly me.

So how can men validate feelings? First, let's define validation. My friend, Darlene Corbett, LICSW, is a Keynote Speaker, Author, Licensed Therapist/Hypnotherapist. She told me that validation is the recognition and acceptance of another person's thoughts, feelings, emotions, and actions as understandable. In lay-person's terms, "I understand why you are (upset or happy)." You aren't agreeing or trying to fix the issue. That is a big step, but there's more. Stay engaged with what is being said. I defer back to Dr. Kolakowski:

> When your partner tells you about their day or shares their feelings, you stay with them in the moment, honoring their experience. You join their world and see things from their point of view. It's a way of showing you understand and accept their thoughts and feelings just as they are. Research has shown that having these types of interactions with your partner helps your partner feel less upset and less vulnerable, whereas invalidating behaviors do the opposite; they make your partner feel criticized, dismissed, or contempt from you.

Listen to understand, accept how they feel, and offer support, not advice, and above all, don't make the classic guy mistake and say, "Don't feel like that."

SAY WHAT YOU MEAN – DON'T ASSUME HE/SHE KNOWS!

> Why are facts and data important? Because in the absence of data, we will always make up false narratives to support a position.
>
> Brene Brown – *Dare to Lead*

So how does Brene Brown's wisdom apply to personal relationships? If we don't say what we think or what we want, or what we feel, our partner may create a completely false narrative. Your partner is not a mind reader. How many times have you said he/she should know what I want or think, or feel? If you don't tell them, they will draw their own conclusion, which more times than not will be wrong.

Let me give you some examples
A man played a round of golf with some business associates and then planned to meet his wife for dinner at their favorite restaurant. The

couple usually goes to this restaurant for special events. Since it was not their anniversary or her birthday, she wondered what was in store as she dressed for their night out. At the restaurant, the husband was quiet and subdued. He didn't engage in the conversations. His mind was elsewhere. As they headed home, the wife wondered and asked, "Is something wrong?" The husband said, "nothing really," and didn't offer anything else.

When they went to bed, the wife started to think something is wrong. Is he unhappy with me? Did I do something to upset him? Why is he so distant? Is something wrong at work? Is our relationship in trouble? Is he seeing someone else? On the other side of the bed, the husband's thought was, who misses a one-foot putt. The husband could have easily avoided an unpleasant evening by simply telling her, "I am so annoyed with myself. I had a one-foot putt to win the match, and I missed it."

In the movie *The Love of the Game*, Kevin Costner, who played a Hall of Fame level baseball pitcher near the end of his career, and Kelly Preston, his love interest when the team is in New York, had a scene where she came to surprise him in Florida during spring training. When she arrived at Kevin's condo, a very attractive masseuse wearing just a robe walked down the stairs. As Kelly angrily walked away, Kevin ran after her and said something to the effect: "You said the rule was no commitment, no exclusivity, you will live your life, and I should live mine. Those were your rules, not mine!" Kelly's response was: "And you believed that!" Now, it just might be me, but don't you think if both characters had expressed that they loved and cherished each other, this unpleasantness could have been avoided?

I have heard many women say (often about me), "he just doesn't get it" or "he isn't listening or picking up the signs!" Ladies, most men don't pick up on the subtle hints. We don't seem to connect the dots very well. After my divorce, I had this conversation with a female high school friend. She said, "We want you to be involved and engaged. We want you to hear what we say by listening, really listening. Then you will know and understand our wishes or desires and act appropriately."

She told me this story. "When my husband and I were engaged, we were walking past a *See's Candy* store. He said he liked the candy with peanuts, and I said I liked butterscotch chocolate. We didn't go into the store or say anything more about the candy. It was just a passing comment as we walked to the car. The next week he brought me a box of *See's* butterscotch chocolate. I was so impressed that he listened and took what I said to heart. He had a particularly enjoyable night." So, I asked her, "If the guy listens and then does something nice as a result of what you said, he has better sex?" Her response, "It's not like a Pavlov dog thing, but it improves the odds."

I told her it would help if there were a glossary of keywords and their meanings. The following week, she sent me this email with a note: "Frank, this is what I call the 'dumb ass' book.' It is your handbook of words and their associated meaning – now you have no excuse."

1. **"Fine"** - This is the word women use at the end of any argument when they feel they are right but can't stand to hear you argue any longer. It means that you should shut up. (NEVER use "fine" to describe how she looks. This will cause you to have one of those arguments.)

2. **"Five minutes"** - This is half an hour. It is equivalent to the five minutes that your football game is going to last before you take out the trash, so it's an even trade.

3. **"Nothing"** - This really means "something," and you should be on your toes. "Nothing" is usually used to describe the feeling a woman has of wanting to turn you inside out, upside down, and backwards. "Nothing" usually signifies an argument that will last "Five Minutes" and end with the word "Fine."

4. **"Go Ahead"** (with raised eyebrows) - This is NOT permission; it's a dare! If you mistake it for permission, the woman will get upset over "Nothing," and you'll have a "five-minute" discussion that will end with the word "Fine."

5. **"Go Ahead"** (normal eyebrows) - This is not permission, either. It means "I give up" or "do what you want because I don't care." You will get a raised eyebrow "Go Ahead" in just a few minutes, followed by "Nothing" and "Fine," and she will talk to you in about "Five Minutes" when she cools off.

6. **(Loud Sigh)** - This is not actually a word but is still often a verbal statement and is very frequently misunderstood by men. A "Loud Sigh" means she thinks you are a complete idiot and wonders why she is wasting her time standing here and arguing with you over "Nothing."

7. **(Soft Sigh)** - Again, not a word, but still a verbal statement. Soft Sighs are one of the few things that some men actually understand. It means she is momentarily content. Your best bet is not to move or breathe in the hope that the moment will last a bit longer.

8. **"Oh"** - This word-followed by any statement - is trouble. Examples include "Oh, let me get that" or, "Oh, I talked to him about what you were doing last night." If she says "Oh" before a statement, run -- do not walk -- to the nearest exit. Do not try to lie more to get out of it, or you will get a raised eyebrow. "Go ahead," sometimes followed by acts so unspeakable that I can't bring myself to write about them.

9. **"That's Okay"** - This is one of the most dangerous statements a woman can say to a man. "That's Okay" means that she wants to think long and hard before deciding what the penalty will be for whatever you have done. "That's Okay" is often used with the word "Fine" and, in conjunction with a raised eyebrow, "Go Ahead." Once she has had time to plan it out, you are in for some mighty big trouble.

10. **"Please Do"** - This is not a statement. The woman is giving you the chance to come up with an excuse for what you have done. In other words, a chance to get yourself into even more trouble. If you handle this correctly, you shouldn't get a "That's okay."

11. **"Thanks"** - The woman is thanking you. Don't faint, and don't look for hidden meanings. Just say, "you're welcome."

12. **"Thanks a lot"** - This is dramatically different from "Thanks." A woman will say "Thanks A Lot" when she is really pissed off at you. It's usually followed by the Loud Sigh and signifies that you have hurt her in some callous way. Be careful not to ask what is wrong after the Loud Sigh, as she will only say, "Nothing."

13. **"You were right"** – Three words men don't often hear. Just say thank you, and then shut up. Gloating, or "I told you so," may cause her to reach back into her files and drop several occurrences where you were wrong.

I sent her an email back thanking her and asked, "Is there such a book for what men should say?" She sent me the following list from cartoonist *Kate Leth*. This list is filled with a very different array of phrases, including apologies, how to call out other men, and ways to stick up for women who are being silenced.

Good statements for men to practice:

1. **"I'm sorry"** – no explanation needed

2. **"I shouldn't have done that"** – again, no explanation needed

3. **"No problem, goodnight"** – might be good to say after you hear, "You were right."

4. **"Dude, don't say that shit"** – letting a male friend know you don't appreciate the comment he made

5. **"Please continue"** – lean forward and make eye contact which values what is being said.

6. **"She wasn't finished"** – again used when someone interrupts or disregards a woman

7. **"How can I help"** – a genuine and sincere offer of assistance when she is upset or struggling

8. **"Actually, that was her idea"** – give credit and validation

Timing plays a major role here in what we say. Making a statement and looking for a specific reaction and then getting upset when we don't get that reaction is not conducive to a positive connection. We all do it. Showing your partner a picture of a proud moment from your past right after they got off the phone arguing with their cellular carrier's customer service is not likely to result in a happy or excited response. Now you are upset because he/she did not give you the response you expected or wanted. Maybe you respond in kind, something like why do I bother telling you things, and the situation has escalated.

Another example is "Look what I bought." The response is "Nice" when you were expecting unbridled excitement. What if you said, "I am so excited! I have wanted this for quite a while, and I found it today on sale." I am willing to bet the response will be closer to what you were expecting. You were looking for validation of your feeling, and he/she dropped the ball. Many years ago, I was told, "your expectations are yours, not your partner's."

While the concept of validation may seem simple, it can sometimes be a little tricky to execute. Imagine your partner comes home and tells you they are furious because they found out they need to work over the holiday weekend. What is your first reaction? Many of us would feel protective of our spouse or be upset at the situation and have the natural urge to help or fix the situation. You might offer advice on how to solve the problem. While it intuitively feels helpful to give suggestions, this can feel invalidating to your partner. Your partner may not be looking for help with a solution -- they probably have already tried to find ways to solve the problem and might feel even more frustrated in hearing advice, no matter how good your intention.

So how do you effectively listen to and validate your partner? There are a few key components to help guide your conversations. Let's go back to Dr. Kolakowski's article one last time.

1. **Mindful listening is the first component of validation.** This means you really pay attention to what your partner is saying. As difficult as it might be, suspend your own judgments and reactions to the situation or topic. Temporarily let go of the need to advise, change, help or fix the situation. Your own thoughts are put on the back burner; your focus, instead, is on your partner's

current experience. Show you are listening by stopping what you are doing (closing the laptop, turning off the TV), turning to face them, nodding your head, and making eye contact as they talk.

2. **Acknowledging and accepting is the next step in validation.** This means you acknowledge what they've said or what they are feeling. You might say, "I can see you're upset about this," or "You seem discouraged" in response to their news about having to work over the weekend. Rather than trying to cheer your partner up, you allow them space to be upset.

3. **Validating does not equal agreeing.** An important distinction is that you can accept your partner's feelings, but it doesn't mean you need to agree with them. For instance, say that you go to see a movie together. Afterward, you discuss your thoughts about the film. Your partner found it entertaining and funny, while you found it boring and predictable. You might validate their point of view by saying, "It sounds like you really enjoyed the film. It wasn't my favorite, but I can tell that you had fun watching it." In this example, you're acknowledging your partner's enjoyment of something without sharing the same sentiment.

4. **Ask questions.** If your partner presents a problem or difficult situation to you, try to find out more about how they are feeling and what they want by asking open-ended questions. "What do you wish would happen?" "What was your reaction to that?" "How are you feeling about things now?" Gently asking questions to clarify their experience can be very gratifying for them. It shows you care and want to really listen.

5. **Show you understand.** Use validating statements such as, "I would feel that way, too," or "It makes sense to me that you'd feel that way given the circumstances" to let them know you see why they feel the way they do. You can also show validation with non-verbals, such as giving them a hug if they feel lonely, making them a drink if they feel jittery, or giving them space if they need time to think.

In the end, it's about the way you interact and connect together, much more so than what you do together. Connect makes all the difference in your relationship.

WORDS MATTER

With the COVID crisis, the entire world endured a life altering event at the same time. The fear, miscommunication, political rhetoric, outright lies, and personal attacks made this terrible situation worse. What we say and how we say it matters.

COVID has placed a major strain on relationships. The April 2, 2020 issue of Psychology Today ran a story called *2020 More Babies or More Divorces after COVID-19*. Catherine Cohan, Ph.D. wrote:

> *I'm inclined to believe we will see an uptick in divorces resulting from the stress of being confined with our spouses with whom we are not accustomed to spending so much one-on-one time. The lack of freedom and day-to-day struggles, coupled with the emotional and financial fallout, will probably take their toll on marriages.*

In a recent CNBC report, lawyers concurred:

> *"For some, life in lockdown due to the coronavirus may feel similar to holidays like Christmas—but that's not necessarily a good thing, as prolonged periods together can prove to make or break for a relationship," U.K. divorce lawyer Baroness Fiona Shackleton of Belgravia told the U.K.'s parliament. She added, "that lawyers in the sector had predicted a likely rise in divorce rates following 'self-imposed confinement.'"*

Will divorces increase post COVID? We will find out soon enough. 2020 brought a great deal of unwanted change to the world. The COVID crisis, unemployment, looming recession, shelter in place, quarantine, the death of someone we know, working from home, and homeschooling have forced us all to change. Spending 24x7 at home with our spouse/ partner and our children is no picnic in many cases. New patterns and rituals had to be created or adjusted without any real warning. One day we were at work and the kids in school; the next day, we were sheltering at home. No matter how much we love our spouse/partner and children, spending that much time sheltering at home will get on everyone's last nerve.

One thing COVID does offer is the ability to press the reset button. How will we interact with our loved ones? What words and actions will we use when our routines have been so drastically altered?

As my friend Tina Konkin wrote in her book, *How God Used "The Other Woman:"*

Words have the power to heal and the power to destroy. They're either poison or fruit; the choice is up to you. Choose to heal by using words that build up rather than tear down, that bring unity rather than division.

It is frustrating and depressing. But, I have met so many people who are using this time to re-evaluate, reflect, and reinvent their lives and their outlook on life. If you are like most people, there was never time to re-evaluate and reflect. We would get out of bed before sunrise and jump on the treadmill of life that constantly went faster and faster. By the end of the day, we go to bed too exhausted to get any real rest and get up a few hours later to start again. We weren't living; we were existing. I have been there. I felt everything little thing mattered; then I realized very little really matters.

Reading my friend Gina Mazza's book *Everything Matters – Nothing Matters* helped drive that point home.

We now have a choice to strengthen our relationship or let it deteriorate. My first piece of advice is to stop watching the news or limit the news to 30 minutes or less. After 30 minutes, the news is just talking heads beating the same story to death.

Words of encouragement, love, and support during chaos are a major deposit in the "love bank." Breaking up the day to have lunch or a snack and talk with our spouse and children or go for a walk, or play a quick game of cards or a video game will strengthen the relationship bonds. Have a "night out" at home. Instead of wearing sweats and slippers and eating the evening meal on paper plates in front of the TV, have the family get dressed up for a night out. Bring out candles and the "good dishes," actual silverware as opposed to plastic ware, and make the interaction special and personal. Tell stories about your family, heritage, and traditions. If you have children make and sleep in a blanket tent once a week, make popcorn, and watch a movie everyone enjoys. The conversations will be full of excitement, love, and positive words.

Hard times will either draw our relationship closer together or pull it apart. We control the scenario. We make the choice. Make the right one.

FIGHT FAIR

When we are confronted with conflict, it is all too easy to focus exclusively on how we are feeling and how we need to respond. Take a deep breath and shift our attention to what's going outside of ourselves during those heated moments.

Unknown

If there is more than one human being involved in any situation, there will eventually be conflict. As social scientists tell us, conflict is not inherently good or bad. What makes it good or bad is how we respond. Every action that occurs in life triggers an emotion. My colleague, Sara Westbrook, who has spent her life studying the impact of emotions, told me that emotions change choices. Circumstances are going to happen that are not under our control. These circumstances trigger powerful emotions. Now we have a choice. We can choose the knee-jerk reaction and lash out, or we can understand and feel the emotion, accept that we are unhappy or upset, yet choose to be respectful in our actions.

Respectful doesn't mean you aren't upset, or you agree, or you cannot give a strong response, but you choose to collect your thoughts and respond without attacking.

The message in the hit song from the Disney movie *Frozen* is, "let it go." Let is go is also good advice for conflict in relationships. Disagreements will occur. They may well escalate into loud shouting matches. Hurtful things are often said in the heat of the moment. Once the argument is over, it is suggested you let it go and move forward. However, this is much easier said than done. There are those who file away the harsh words or mistakes of their partner and lie in wait to bring them up later. This is pouring gasoline on the fire.

Freelance columnist Julie Compton conducted an interview with married couple therapists Casey and Meygan Caston on Fighting Fair. The article appeared in NBC News' *BETTER* blog on October 2, 2017. The article summarized five points:

1. **Keep your cool**. This is key to fighting fair. When we feel the emotions of the moment are getting too heated, take a break. This is a common practice in business during high-stakes negotiations. Again, much easier said than done; however, it is far better to have a cooling down period than to cross a line that cannot be uncrossed.

2. **Be polite**. When we interrupt, we are listening to respond rather than understand. We are also trying to control the conversation. To prevent interrupting, choose an object and make it a rule that only the person holding it can speak. (Note: if you use this one, please make sure the object you select will not cause harm to either party or household items if thrown. Been there!!)

3. **Focus on the present**. Focus only on the argument at hand. When fights start to get ugly, it's tempting to bring up past grievances. So, let's avoid the incident at the Christmas party three years ago.

4. **Don't lash out**. When fights get dirty, couples start to name call. This turns the attention away from the problem and focuses on the person instead.

5. Say you're sorry. Apologizing is often the quickest way to resolve a conflict. But to work, it needs to be done properly. An effective apology acknowledges the hurt you've caused, accepts responsibility for it and asks for forgiveness.

Once again, in the heat of the moment, rules tend to be pushed to the wayside. I know I've done it, and several personal relationships evaporated. The result is I, and many of us become more hardened and calloused and will likely fail again. Here are two quotes by Albert Einstein that might help us:

1. The definition of insanity is "doing the same thing over and over again but expecting different results."

2. "We cannot solve our problems with the same thinking we used when we created them."

As we saw earlier, we cannot separate our personal life from our professional life. The people who have found a way to be happy and successful in both are rare and truly blessed. It comes down to accountability. We will touch on this is the next and final chapter.

Stepping Stones for Business Success

1. **Communicate to make connections**
2. **Grand gestures are nice, but the consistency of word and deed mean far more**
3. **People aren't mind readers – say what you mean**
4. **Words matter**
5. **Fight Fair**

CHAPTER 22

Accountability in our Personal Relationships

"Take accountability... Blame is the water in which many dreams and relationships drown."

Steve Maraboli

Relationships are hard. They take far more work and effort than most believe and many are willing to make. Landmines are lurking at every turn. What are they? Where are they? When will they arrive? Is there a roadmap so we can avoid them? We all want the fairy tale ending, the happily ever after story, the dream relationship, right? The first step is finding that someone, whom you are willing and he/she is willing to make some type of commitment. This process is more daunting than we may expect. It is commonly referred to as dating hell. Hell is not usually associated with something good. We have all heard the dating pep talks from well-meaning friends and family; you have to kiss a lot of frogs before you find that prince or princess; there are a lot of fish in the sea; the right one will come along when you least expect it.

Now, if you are lucky enough to make your way through the frogs and the fish and actually find someone, you start down the happily ever after trail. Then life happens. Student loan payments start, rent, food, bills start to pile up. Maybe you started grad school that will accumulate more debt. Maybe the relationship evolved into marriage and children;

priorities changed again. Hopefully, you were able to turn a job into a career that pays the bills, allows you to put away some money, buy a car, a house, raise a family, take an occasional vacation, and buy the "toys" that make you happy. Your career becomes more and more demanding. More hours, more time away, less being present, and more stress and strain on the relationship. If you are not careful, life becomes a grind where you exist rather than live. Then the doubts set in. Am I really happy? Is this what I signed up for?

The common denominator in all my relationships that did not end well is me. I am not a celebrity or sports hero or a national or even local politician or business tycoon. I am not a Ph.D. or counselor or psychologist, or self-help guru. I am an average American man who gets up every day and does the best he can to love, nurture, protect and support my family. I try to do whatever it takes. Sometimes that means working long hours or two jobs or being on the road. Most times, the strain from my professional life led to the downfall of my personal relationships. This is not an excuse or a way to justify my failed relationships. Since I am the common denominator, I must hold myself accountable. I cannot control every obstacle life throws at me. I can control if and how I let these obstacles affect me. It is up to me to reflect on my thoughts, words, and deeds and redirect them, so I have the opportunity to become one of those rare and blessed people who enjoys a positive professional and personal life.

Remember this, none of us are in this alone. The secret to walking on water is to know where the rocks are. Take the time to read and answer the workbook questions at the end of this book. Discuss them with your friends, colleagues, and family. If you like, contact me, and I will hold a workshop.

Stepping Stones for Business Success

1. **Be accountable**
2. **The common denominator in your failed relationships is you**

Addendum 1

TAG TEAM APPLICATION

Congratulations. By downloading and completing this application, you are taking the first step toward building, scaling and sustaining a successful organization. The TAG TEAM (TT) will select three entities per year with the most unique products/services with the highest revenue and profit potential. You can download this application at https://www/frankzaccari.com

Please submit your Executive Summary. TT will respond within five business days with comments and questions. After receiving your updated submission, we will set up a call to determine the next steps.

Customer Problem: Why are you starting the business?

1. What is the customer pain, and how does the company solve it (concept & key elements?) Does it pass the "who cares" test?

2. Product Overview: Explain what the company does, for whom and why it's compelling?

3. Key Players: Who are the founders, key team members, and key advisers? Include industry backgrounds and expertise. How much skin do they have in the game?

4. Market Opportunity: Who wants or needs this product/service? What are the market size, growth characteristics, and segmentation? No product or service addresses every part of a market. What is your sweet spot?

5. Competitive Landscape: Who are your competitors and competitive feature sets? Why and how is competition failing to service this market? Why do you think you will? What are your

sustainable competitive advantages? Will you be able to scale? How?

6. Go-To-Market Strategy: How will the company sell its product/service? Explain in detail, including how much it will cost to build that sales engine.

7. Stage of Development: How far along is the product? Be honest! Is development complete? If not, how much time, energy and money are needed to get to prototype or pilot? What customers have evaluated the product? What is their feedback? Who are you partnering with for customer acquisition, partner relationships, etc.?

8. Critical Risks & Challenges: What can go wrong, and how the company plans to manage it? (Top developer leaves, addressing delays getting approvals, certifications, permits, etc.)

9. Financial Projections: How much time and money will it take to get to cash flow break-even? Has an accountant/financial person prepared a five-year projection (it is really helpful if entrepreneurs show Year 5 mid-case, worst case, and best case with key assumptions)?

10. Funding Requirements: How much money does the company need to launch this product into the market? When do you need the money? What is it going to be used for – be specific? What milestones you expect and when? When do you project profitability?

This is the 1st step. If you pass this initial screening, additional details will be drawn out during subsequent Q&A or subsequent due diligence. If you qualify, TT is here to help you.

Send your response to frankzaccari@gmail.com

Addendum 2

THE RECOMMENDED PROCESS

The Mission: TAG TEAM is creating it's its own line of startups with the potential to attain revenues of over $100M in 5 years with at least 25% profitability. We will limit acceptance to three organizations per year.

The Process: THE TAG TEAM will work with the leading research universities and other institutions to identify, screen, evaluate, qualify, and provide expertise to promising start-up and/or early phase organizations. The focus will be on innovative and disruptive organizations primarily from the medical/green industries. Potential organizations will complete a rigorous application and screening process, which will include but not be limited to:

1. The management team's credentials, background, strengths, and weaknesses
2. Completion of THE TAG TEAM executive summary request
3. Business plan
   a. Sales
   b. Marketing
   c. Operations
   d. Finance
   e. Growth Strategy
4. Funding already in place – must be properly funded through existing sources or from funding arranged by THE TAG TEAM
5. Revenue stream
6. Expenses

7. Additional funding needed to launch and scale, use of funds and milestones

If accepted, THE TAG TEAM will provide a "SWAT TEAM" of proven professionals to fill in the skills and knowledge gap as needed. THE TAG TEAM will oversee the day-to-day operation, allowing the founders to focus on their strengths. Once the organization has met the screening and qualification requirements, they will be introduced to The Abraham Group (TAG), headed by Jay Abraham, who will develop a "success roadmap in conjunction with THE TAG TEAM and the organization." THE TAG TEAM will then work with and monitor the organization's process adhering to the success roadmap. Subject matter experts will be added as needed to keep the organization on the plan and/or make adjustments. Once the startup meets THE TAG TEAM's rigorous criteria, exponential growth and profitability will be expected. The organization and THE TAG TEAM will have an equity and revenue sharing model where the synergy of our skills will result in the optimum level of success.

Benefits to All Stakeholders:

- Startup Founders - Monetizing (IP) products/services and retaining higher equity while focusing on core strengths, R&D, etc.
- University – Equity/or receive scholarships in valuable enterprise and enhanced reputation
- Marketplace - Innovative medical/green solutions at lower costs.
- THE TAG TEAM - Consulting clients accelerate the entry and success of new and innovative companies into the marketplace.

Acknowledgments

First and foremost, my daughters Stephanie and Sara have been my inspiration since the day they were born, and my grandchildren Casen and Cashlynn brings us all more joy than we deserve. My wife Helen, and Sean, who I consider my son. Helen believed in me when I didn't believe in myself.

It took many years of good and bad experiences to write this book. After selling my company in 2016, I started to leverage the knowledge and experience I gained to help aspiring entrepreneurs and other leaders uncover hidden opportunities and find solutions to pressing personal and professional challenges. This journey gave me the opportunity to teach a workshop for aspiring entrepreneurs at Arizona State University; become a mentor with the Veterans Treatment Court; a mentor and judge with the University of California Entrepreneurship Academy; co-found THE TAG TEAM program with Jay Abraham and Gaby Ory; be one of the designers with Julio Alvarado for a non-profit group Awakening Wholeness Inc; became a featured contributor for West Coast Magazine, VOCAL and BIZCATALYST 360; and host a weekly radio and TV show, Life Altering Events, which in one year had over 200,000 listeners in 42 countries.

I have met and now call friends some of the most dynamic, interesting, intelligent, and truly amazing people. Along the way, I learned to mellow my hard-driving Type A personality and can connect with people on a personal level. This would not have happened without all the people that have entered my life. This includes my voiceamerica.

com support teams. The guests whom I had the privilege to interview: Mina and Adrian Perez, Kimberly Hobscheid, Mel Robbins, Latachia Morrissette Harper, Steve Zaccari, Annette Zaccari, Dr. Leonard Abbeduto, Dr. Julie Schweitzer, Dr. July Van de Water, The Honorable David Abbot, Cindy Baldwin, Dr. Marc Porter, Susanna Bravo, Jim McLaughlin, Dr. Andrew Hargadon, Dr. Maria Artunduaga, Mark Balzer, Nicole Bendaly, Julio Alvarado, Dr. Sara McClellan, Rebecca Graulich, Benjamin Pyles, Dr. Ruth Lee, Dr. Vernet Joseph, Matt Johnson, Kimberly Johnson, Tom Crea, Tony Vitrano, Sam Altawil, JD, Mary Peddy, Sandra Pieszak, Remy Meraz, Susan Golden, Nico Marcolongo, Myra Bennet, Rev. Ariel Patricia, Kathleen O'Keefe-Kanavos, Teresa Velardi, Charon King, Shin Ae Kook, Ryan Dovich, Dan Epstein, Joseph Molina, Darryl Gooden, Kelly Anne Wilde, Lorde Astor West, Dr. Stephanie Red Feather, Olivia Russo-Hood, Christopher Taylor, Dr. Bonnie McLean, Dr. Larry Burk, Miguel Dean, Robert Willis, David Woods Bartley, Tina Konkin, Dr. Clare Hasler-Lewis, Claudia Baier Vogas, Dr. Natasha Todorovic-Cowen, Heidi Boucher, David Nassaney, Gina Gardiner, Lisa Byres, Laura Staley, Dr. Dena Samuels, Dr. Teri Slack, Katherine Hu, Gina Mazza, Jackie Simmons, Steve Eriksen, Ana Billian, Harold Mintz, Dean Eller, Dr. Temple Hayes, Ken Walls, Mike Pitocco, Connie Bramer, Eileen Bild, Darlene Corbett, Belinda Farrell, Sarah McVanel, Sara Westbrook, Megan Fenyoe, Sarah Lawrence, Betty Brink, Dominique Brightmton, Michele Starwalt-Woods, Frannie Matthews Ilene Dillion, Carolyn Lebanoski, JoAnna Bennett, Susan Rooks, Jeff Ikler, Cindy Cline, Teresa Quinlan, Edward Hess, Richard Dugan, Elizabeth Welles, Dr. Shelley Kaehr, Regan Forston, Mark O'Brien, John Mathis, Maria Lehtman, Roberta Moore, Shelly Harrison and Lauren Ward Larsen. Each of your stories enriched my life and the lives of people all over the world.

End Notes

Chapter 1: Everything you want is on the other side of fear

- Don Miguel Ruiz – The Four Agreements, Amber-Allen Publishing, Incorporated (July 10, 2018)

Chapter 2: Do you have the courage to get what you want

- Brene Brown – Dare to Lead, VERMILION (October 11, 2018)
- Mel Robbins – The Five Second Rule, Independently published (July 11, 2019)

Chapter 3 Do you know what you don't know

- Steve Lamoureux - The Fallacy of Instinct: Common Pitfalls to Avoid When Making Design Decisions January 26, 2018
- Netflix subscribers count in the U.S. | Statistawww.statista.com Jan 13, 2021).
- Tiffany Hsu - The World's Last Blockbuster Has No Plans to Close, New York Times (March 6, 2019)
- "The Decision Loom: A Design for Interactive Decision-Making in Organizations," Vince Barabba, Triarchy Press Ltd (November 24, 2011)
- Tom Crea – Unleash Your Values, Independently published August 12, 2016
- Edward Hess - Hyper-Learning: How to Adapt at the Speed of Change, Berrett-Koehler Publishers (September 1, 2020)

- J. Bruce Tracey, Timothy R. Hinkin, Thao Li Bui Tran, A Field Study of New Employee Training Programs: Industry Practices and Strategic Insights - Training Industry Quarterly (November 5, 2014)
- Greenleaf Center for Servant Leadership, https://www.greenleaf.org/what-is-servant-leadership/
- Britannica – www.britannica.com

Chapter 4 – What is Normal

- Edward Hess - Hyper-Learning: How to Adapt at the Speed of Change, Berrett-Koehler Publishers (September 1, 2020)
- The Harvard Business Review article August 7, 2020 by Ashish K. Bhatia and Natalia Levina

Chapter 5 - Imagination or Intelligence

Chapter 6—Best Practice or Next Practice

- Frank Zaccari – Presentation – Imagination or Intelligence
- Simon Sinek – The Infinite Game, Portfolio (October 15, 2019)
- Brene Brown – Dare to Lead, VERMILION (October 11, 2018)

Chapter 7—The Importance of Collaboration

- John Donahoe - Quote - https://www.inspiringquotes.us/author/5636-john-donahoe
- John P. Kotter – Leading Change, Harvard Business Review Press; 1R edition (November 6, 2012)
- Mark Balzer – The People Principles, AuthorHouse (June 2011)
- Matthew Neill Davis - The Art of Preventing Stupid, An, Incorporated Original (April 2019)
- Fortune Magazine – Fortune (May 2017)

Chapter 8 – Changing a Culture

- James Kouzes/Barry Posner – The Leadership Challenge, Jossey-Bass; 6th edition (April 17, 2017)

- John P. Kotter – Leading Change, Harvard Business Review Press; 1R edition (November 6, 2012)
- Kimberly Davis - Brave Leadership, Greenleaf Book Group Press (January 16, 2018)
- Jim Collins - Good to Great, HarperBusiness; 1st edition (October 16, 2001)
- Daniel Pink - The Surprising Truth About What Motivates Us https://www.ted.com/talks/dan_pink_the_puzzle_of_motivation
- Daniel Pink – Ted Talk https://www.ted.com/talks/dan_pink_ the_puzzle_of_motivation
- Sam Altawil - On The Edge of Effectiveness – Refocusing HR Efforts To Strengthen Organizations, Independently published (April 10, 2019)

Chapter 9—Creating Long Term Success

- Frank Zaccari - From the Ashes: The Rise of the University of Washington Volleyball Program, CreateSpace Independent Publishing Platform (October 10, 2010)
- Jim Collins – Great by Choice, Harper Business; 1st edition (October 11, 2011)
- Jim Collins - How the Mighty Fall, Jim Collins; 1st edition (May 19, 2009)
- Tom Rath and Barry Conchie - Strengths Based Leadership, Gallup Press; 1st edition (January 1, 2008)
- Steve Jobs Quote, https://www.themuse.com/advice/25-steve-jobs-quotes-that-will-change-the-way-you-workin-the-best-way-possible

Chapter 10 – Won't work in my organization

- Kerry Patterson, Joseph Grenny, Ron McMillan, Al Switzler – Crucial Conversations: Tools for Talking When Stakes Are High, McGraw-Hill Education; 2nd edition (September 7, 2011)

- Dave Asprey – Game Changers, Harper Wave; Illustrated edition (December 4, 2018)
- Jim Collins – How the Mighty Fall, Jim Collins; 1st edition (May 19, 2009)
- Tom Rath & Barry Conchie – Strength Based Leadership, Gallup Press; 1st edition (January 1, 2008)

Chapter 11— Is the Under Ground Harming Your Business?

- Kerry Patterson, Joseph Grenny, Ron McMillan, Al Switzler – Crucial Conversations, Gallup Press; 1st edition (January 1, 2008)
- Marc Porter Ph.D – Common Ground – from the book by Cynthia King – Creating Partnerships, Wisdom Way Press (May 1, 2005)
- Bain & Company, Gallup, Eastern Kentucky University – Employee Engagement Study, https://www.gallup.com/workplace/
- Don Miguel Ruiz - The Four Agreements, Amber-Allen Publishing, Incorporated (July 10, 2018)
- Kimberly Davis – Brave Leadership, Greenleaf Book Group Press (January 16, 2018)
- Brene Brown – Dare to Lead, VERMILION (October 11, 2018)
- Dr. Laura Staley - Live Alive, Sacred Stories Publishing (March 23, 2020)
- Simon Sinek - Leaders Eat, Portfolio; Illustrated edition (January 7, 2014)
- Michael Fullan - Leading in a Culture of Change, Jossey-Bass; Revised edition (February 2, 2007)

Chapter 12—Are You Communicating or Connecting

- Nicole Bendaly – Winner Instinct, iUniverse; Revised edition (January 21, 2019)
- Mark Balzer – The People Principles, AuthorHouse (June 2011)
- Brene Brown – Dare to Lead, VERMILION (October 11, 2018)

- Don Miguel Ruiz – The Four Agreements, Amber-Allen Publishing, Incorporated (July 10, 2018)
- Kerry Patterson, Joseph Grenny, Ron McMillan, Al Switzler – Crucial Conversations, Gallup Press; 1st edition (January 1, 2008)

Chapter 13 – Finding the Right People

- Quote from Henry Mintzberg, https://www.azquotes.com/author/10183-Henry_Mintzberg
- Dr. Angela Duckworth - Grit, The Power of Passion and Persistence, Scribner Book Company; 1st edition (May 1, 2016)
- Simon Sinek - youtube talk https://www.youtube.com/watch?v=zP9jpxitfb4
- Simon Sinek - Leaders Eat Last, Portfolio; Illustrated edition (January 7, 2014)
- Roland Busch - Inc Magazine Interview, (Jul 27, 2020)
- Daniel Coyle – Culture Code, Random House Audio; Unabridged edition (January 30, 2018)
- Dr. Dena Samuels – Mindfulness Effect, Night River Press; 1st edition (August 6, 2018)

Chapter 14— The New Breed of Innovators

- Geralyn Hurd - a partner at the accounting, consulting and technology firm Crowe
- Bill Burnett and Dave Evans - Designing Your Life, Knopf; Illustrated edition (September 20, 2016)
- David Asprey - Game Changers, Illustrated edition (December 4, 2018)
- Frannie Matthews - Mom, I just eliminated my own job, – LinkedIn article
- Carol S. Dweck – Mindset: The New Psychology of Success, Ballantine Books; Updated Edition (December 26, 2007)

Chapter 15— Press the Reset Button

- Nicole Bendaly – Winner Instinct, iUniverse; Revised edition (January 21, 2019)
- Brene Brown – Dare to Lead, VERMILION (October 11, 2018)
- Harvard Business Review, August 14, 2020 Nirmalya Kumar and Koen Pauwels - Don't Cut Your Marketing Budget in a Recession

Chapter 16 – Ask for What You Need

- Jay Abraham quote - https://www.goodreads.com/author/quotes/51660.Jay_Abraham
- Simon Sinek – Start with Why, Portfolio; Illustrated edition (December 27, 2011)

Chapter 17 – Life is More Than Making a Living

- Gina Mazza – Everything Matters, Nothing Matters, St. Lynn's Press (April 1, 2008)
- Brene Brown – Dare to Lead, VERMILION (October 11, 2018)
- Dave Asprey – Game Changers, Illustrated edition (December 4, 2018)
- Janet and Chris Attwood - The Passion Test, Gildan Media (Sep 15, 2006)
- Lauren Ward Larsen – Zuzu's Petals, In The Telling Press; First Edition (November 25, 2010)

Chapter 18 - Personal Life Landmines

- Steven Covey - https://www.brainyquote.com/authors/stephen-covey-quotes
- Robby Benson - BigThink.com - https://bigthink.com/robby-berman
- Alice Boyes Ph.D. - Psychology Today, (September 21, 2018)

Chapter 19— How Did We Get Here

- Maya Angelou - Quote - https://www.google.com/search?q=quotes+from+maya+angelou
- Webster's New World Dictionary 2nd edition - Toxic Masculinity Definition
- Women in Congress - Pew Research – (January 15,2021)
- Fortune 500 Women CEOs - Fortune Magazine (August 4, 2020)
- Dorothy W. Hartman – Lives of Women in Connor Prairie - https://www.connerprairie.org/
- Inc Magazine August 2019 – Gender Pay Gap
- Cheri Preston – – Women in Business - ABC News interview WTMJ News (October 22, 2019)
- Gender Roles and Stereo Types - Planned Parenthood article – https://www.plannedparenthood.org/learn/gender-identity/sex-gender-identity/what-are-gender-roles-and-stereotypes

Chapter 20 — Leave Work at Work

- Frank Zaccari – When the Wife Cheats, Create Space Independent Publishing Platform (July 21, 2010)
- Kim Scott – Radical Candor, Macmillan Audio –(March 14, 2017)

Chapter 21—Dialogue Requires Deep Listening

- Quote from Epictetus - https://www.goodreads.com/author/quotes/13852.Epictetus
- Nicole Bendaly – Winner Instinct - iUniverse; Revised edition (January 21, 2019)
- Dr. Shannon Kolakowski - HuffPost 11/20/2012
- Love of the Game - Movie reference, Distributed by Universal Pictures (September 17, 1999)

- Kath Leth – List of statement men should say – from Comic Kath Leth
- Dr. Catherine Cohen – 2020 More Babies or Divorces after Covid - Psychology Today, (April 2, 2020)
- Vicky McKeever -CNBC Report – More Divorces after Covid? – (Mar 25 2020)
- Tina Konkin – How God Used The Other Woman, Focus on the Family (July 9, 2019)
- Gina Mazza – Everything Matters, Nothing Matters, St. Lynn's Press (April 1, 2008)
- Frozen - Movie reference, Distributed by Walt Disney Studios Home Entertainment (November 18, 2014)
- Meygan Caston – Fighting Fair - NBC News Better Blog – (October 2, 2017)

Chapter 22 -Accountability in our Personal Relationships

- Steve Marabelo quote from - https://www.google.com/search?q =quote+from+steve+maraboli

Additional Reading

Other Books by Frank Zaccari

1. *When the Wife Cheats* – CreateSpace Independent Publishing Platform (July 21, 2010) Frank Zaccari (Author)

2. *From the Ashes - The Rise of the University of Washington Volleyball Program* – CreateSpace Independent Publishing Platform (October 10, 2010) Frank Zaccari (Author)

3. *Inside the Spaghetti Bowl* – CreateSpace Independent Publishing Platform (September 27, 2011), Frank Zaccari (Co-Author), Anthony Zaccari (Co-Author), Steven Zaccari (Co-Author)

4. *Five Years to Live* – CreateSpace Independent Publishing Platform (September 24, 2012), Frank Zaccari (Co-Author), Anthony Zaccari (Co-Author), Steven Zaccari (Co-Author)

5. *Storm Seeds* – CreateSpace Independent Publishing Platform (October 28, 2013), Frank Zaccari (Co-Author), Anthony Zaccari (Co-Author), Steven Zaccari (Co-Author)

6. *Crappy to Happy* – Sacred Stories Publishing (November 20, 2019), Kathleen O'Keefe-Kanavos (Co-Author), Rev. Patricia Cagganello (Co-Author), Bernie Sioegel M.D. (Foreward), Frank Zaccari, Deborah J. Beauvais, Constance Bramer, Tamara Knox, Kristi Tornabene, Teresa Velardi, Dominique Brightmon, (Co-Authors), Amazon Best Seller

Other Special Authors

1. *The Four Agreements* - Amber-Allen Publishing, Incorporated (July 10, 2018), Don Miguel Ruiz (Author)

2. *Dare to Lead*, VERMILION (October 11, 2018), Brene Brown (Author)

3. *The Five Second Rule*, Independently published (July 11, 2019), Mel Robbins (Author)

4. *The Infinite Game* - Portfolio (October 15, 2019), Simon Sinek (Author)

5. *Leading Change* - Harvard Business Review Press; 1R edition (November 6, 2012), John P. Kotter (Author)

6. *The People Principles* – AuthorHouse (June 2011), Mark Balzer (Author)

7. *The Art of Preventing Stupid* - An, Incorporated Original (April 2019), Matthew Neill Davis (Author)

8. *The Leadership Challenge* - Jossey-Bass; 6th edition (April 17, 2017), James Kouzes/Barry Posner (Authors)

9. *Brave Leadership* - Greenleaf Book Group Press (January 16, 2018), Kimberly Davis (Author)

10. *Good to Great* - Good to Great, HarperBusiness; 1st edition (October 16, 2001), Jim Collins (Author)

11. *Great by Choice* - Harper Business; 1st edition (October 11, 2011), Jim Collins (Author)

12. *How the Mighty Fall* - 1st edition (May 19, 2009), Jim Collins (Author)

13. *Strengths Based Leadership* - Gallup Press; 1st edition (January 1, 2008), Tom Rath and Barry Conchie (Authors)

14. *Crucial Conversations* - Gallup Press; 1st edition (January 1, 2008) Kerry Patterson, Joseph Grenny, Ron McMillan, Al Switzler (Authors)

15. *Winner Instinct* - iUniverse; Revised edition (January 21, 2019), Nicole Bendaly (Author)

16. *Live Alive* - Sacred Stories Publishing (March 23, 2020), Dr. Laura Staley (Author)

17. *Leaders Eat Last Leaders Eat* - Portfolio; Illustrated edition (January 7, 2014), Simon Sinek (Author)

18. *Leading in a Culture of Change* - Jossey-Bass; Revised edition (February 2, 2007), Michael Fullan (Author)

19. *Grit, The Power of Passion and Persistence* - Scribner Book Company; 1st edition (May 1, 2016), Dr. Angela Duckworth (Author)

20. *Culture Code* - Random House Audio; Unabridged edition (January 30, 2018), Daniel Coyle (Author)

21. *Mindfulness Effect* - Night River Press; 1st edition (August 6, 2018), Dr. Dena Samuels (Author)

22. *Designing Your Life* - Knopf; Illustrated edition (September 20, 2016), Bill Burnett and Dave Evans (Authors)

23. *Game Changers* - Illustrated edition (December 4, 2018), David Asprey (Author)

24. *Mindset: The New Psychology of Success,* Ballantine Books; Updated Edition (December 26, 2007), Carol S. Dweck (Author)

25. *Everything Matters, Nothing Matters* - St. Lynn's Press (April 1, 2008), Gina Mazza (Author)
The Passion Test - Gildan Media (Sep 15, 2006), Janet Attwood and Chris Attwood (Authors)

26. Zuzu's Petals, In The Telling Press; First Edition (November 25, 2010), Lauren Ward Larsen (Author)
The Decision Loom: A Design for Interactive Decision-Making in Organizations - Triarchy Press Ltd (November 24, 2011), Vince Barabba (Author)

Unleash Your Values - Independently published (August 12, 2016), Tom Crea (Author)

27. *Hyper-Learning: How to Adapt at the Speed of Change* - Berrett-Koehler Publishers (September 1, 2020), Edward Hess (Author)

28. *Start with Why* - Portfolio; Illustrated edition (December 27, 2011), Simon Sinek (Author)

29. *On The Edge of Effectiveness – Refocusing HR Efforts To Strengthen Organizations* - Independently published (April 10, 2019), Sam Altawil (Author)
Radical Candor - Macmillan Audio (March 14, 2017), Kim Scott (Author)

30. *How God Used The Other Woman* - Focus on the Family (July 9, 2019), Tina Konkin (Author)

Business Secrets for Walking on Water WorkBook and Book Club Questions

Business Secrets to Walking on Water is an ideal source for Master's clubs, networking groups, company management training meetings, university organizational development, sociology or business management classes, and book club discussions. Why? Because at times, it seems like creating, expanding, and sustaining a happy personal and professional life is like trying to walk on water. It can be done if you know the secret.

The majority of the people who buy and discuss Walking on Water have attained a fair amount of success; however, professional success often takes a devastating toll on our personal life. Now, if you grew up like me, you were told to put in the effort, energy, time, make sacrifices because, in the end, your family will reap the benefits. Good in theory, right? Not so good in reality. Regardless of how smart we are, how much industry knowledge we have, how many hours we work to master our craft, we are never going to know it all. One of the major problems most leaders face is we over-extend ourselves. We try to juggle twenty balls at once, and unfortunately, most of the balls hit the ground. So, what do we do? We work harder and longer. This makes things worse. We spend more and more time away from home, and even when we are home, we aren't present. Our minds are elsewhere. We convince ourselves we are doing this for our family, but what the family sees is time with them isn't important. We are not fully involved and engaged. The home life suffers, and our professional life suffers.

We find ourselves in a battle between time and money. We might say I am happy making $200,000 a year, but our logical mind says you would be twice as happy if you made $400,000. So, we follow our logical brain. We trade time for money. The less time we have, the fewer memories we make with our spouse and children. As I wrote in Chapter 17, no one says that they wish they had spent more time in the office on their death bed. Things go away or can be taken away (job, title, house, big income, car, vacation home), but memories last forever. As you get together with your children, grandchildren, and spouse, the happy memories are when you did things together.

I hope as you read and discuss Walking on Water, you will come to the realization that what you know is not nearly as important as what you don't know. What you don't know in your personal and professional life is what will sink you. Talk about what you don't know and what you don't like doing. Commit yourself to work with organizations like the TAG TEAM to bring the expertise you lack in certain areas. You will read about many of the obstacles I faced and read from experts about avoiding or overcoming these obstacles that we often never see coming. The secret to walking on water is to know where the rocks are.

I have left space for you to record your thoughts, reactions, and plans to discover what you don't know. I have included discussion points by chapter. I would love to hear your thoughts, suggestions, and comments. Contact me, and I will set up a workshop for your organization.

Introduction

1. What demons are you battling?
2. Are you really engaged and involved in your personal and professional life?
3. What really matters to you?
4. What was the 2x4 that hit you between the eyes?

Chapter 1 Everything You Want is on the Other Side of Fear

1. Be prepared to face your fears. As Joseph Campbell wrote: The cave you fear to enter holds the treasure you seek. What is your cave?

2. "I didn't have the opportunity" is not a reason or an excuse. It's a choice. What opportunity are you looking for?

3. Don't settle. What do you really want?

4. How are you going to choose to be a participant in your life or a spectator?

Chapter 2 Do You Have the Courage To Get What You Want

1. What is your passion? Write it down. If you don't know what it is, we will discover it.

2. Be engaged and involved. Life, or God, or the universe is giving you signs. It starts with a touch, then a tap, then a push, and finally a 2X4 between the eyes. What signs have you been ignoring?

3. Be ready to take the 1st step. MLK said, "Faith is taking the 1st step even when you can't see the whole staircase. What 1st step do you need to take?

4. Stop worrying about how you are going to get there. Start moving forward, and the how will become apparent. If something is meant to be, the doors will open, and you will see the path to follow. What doors are opening for you?

Chapter 3 Do You Know What You Don't Know

1. What people are you bringing in as strategic partners? Have they been there and done that? Be honest. I am not talking about your frat brother who wrote an app. I am talking about people who have started, scaled, financed, and sustained an organization.

2. Survival belongs to those who are able to adjust and adapt to change. Are you adapting?

3. Are you developing a servant leadership mindset?

4. The world is changing at hyper-speed, and we must develop hyper-learning to keep up. Are you able to learn, unlearn and relearn?

Chapter 4 What is Normal

1. Great leaders are the ones who think beyond "short term" vs. "long term." What is your long-term objective?

2. Your old normal is gone. What adjustments are you making personally and professionally?

3. How old is your "best practice?" Write down two potential next practices. What will it take to deploy these next practices?

4. In what areas do you struggle? How are you addressing these areas?

Chapter 5 Imagination or Intelligence

1. What things are within reach by just learning and putting one foot in front of the other?

2. When have you found "Imagination is more important than intelligence?"

3. Does your vision paint a picture people can see, understand and follow? How do you know?

4. Imagination and vision need direction for success. It helps to ask a few strategic questions. What questions are you asking? Who are you asking?

Chapter 6 Best Practice or Next Practice

1. Best practices are a point in time. They are not gospel and should be challenged. How often are you reviewing and adjusting?

2. The companies that change the world find the "next practice." What steps are you taking?

3. Innovation can come from anyone in the organization – be listening. How are you encouraging your staff?

Chapter 7 The Importance of Collaboration

1. Get out of the weeds. Stop working in your business and start working on your business. What should you be delegating?

2. How are you working with people/groups to complement your skills and abilities?

3. Examine your culture. It is more important than your strategy or products – get it right. Write down your culture in one sentence.

4. Self-sabotage is more common than one would believe. What signs of self-sabotage do you see?

5. Most organizations die from suicide. Poor choices, poor hires, poor processes, poor attitudes are all self-inflicted wounds. What danger signs do you see?

6. Do a self-assessment or have a 3rd party perform one.

Chapter 8 Changing a Culture

1. No one likes change. Great leaders explain why and then model how to change. How do you explain and model change?

2. When implementing change, remember it will get harder before it gets easier. Stay the course. What small victories have you celebrated?

3. Lead through a lens of humanity. People cannot leave their emotions at the door. How are you encouraging meaningful dialogue?

4. Your focus must be on addressing the needs of others – this will build trust. Without trust, you will fail. What steps are you taking to know and understand the needs of your employees, co-workers, and customers?

Chapter 9 Creating Long Term Success

1. Great opportunities come from great adversity. How are you pressing the reset button?

2. Have a vision that you believe in, explain the vision, and have total commitment to the Vision. The vision doesn't change, but your tactics have to change with the times. What tactics have you changed? Why did you need to change the tactics?

3. Discipline, in essence, is consistency of action. What are your core values?

Chapter 10 My Organization is Unique, Your Plan Will Not Work Here

1. Different industries have more in common than they think. Your issues are not all that unique. List what keeps you awake at night.

2. Review if or how you are implementing the 10 Steps?

3. You will find what you are looking for. Are you looking for success? How? What are you finding? If you are looking for why something will fail, it will fail.

Chapter 11 Is the Underground Harming Your Business

1. The majority of employees are not engaged at work. Take the blind poll outlined in this chapter. The results may surprise you.

2. Fear and lack of trust are a deadly combination for employment-related lawsuits. How are you improving trust and making connections in your company?

3. Conflict is inevitable, but by creating an environment of mutual respect, conflict does not have to become contentious. What words are being used in your business?

Chapter 12 – Are You Communicating or Connecting

1. Trust must be earned every day. How do you engage at work and home?

2. Words matter. What are the words you hear most often in your organizations?

3. Communicate with the intention of forming a connection. What processes are you using to make a real connection with people?

Chapter 13 – Finding the Right People

1. A new recruiting model based on character traits and soft skills is needed. Do your job descriptions address character?

2. Look for people with passion and persistence (Grit). "Grinders" usually work out better than people with natural skills. How are you identifying the grinders?

3. How are you nurturing strong team players, not heroes?

Chapter 14 – The New Breed of Innovators

1. Don't believe me, just watch – Are you constantly asking, "what if?" Give three examples.

2. Find opportunities where others find problems. Name two in your business or personal life.

3. Creativity, execution, feedback, and iteration are the cornerstones of success in this dynamic world. Does your family or employees feel safe looking for new alternatives?

Chapter 15 Press the Reset Button

1. Act...Don't React. What steps have you taken personally and professionally during challenging times?

2. Be prepared to press the reset button. The only constant is change. Are you prepared? How are you preparing?

3. You don't know how strong you are until strong is your only option. Give three examples of how you have picked yourself up and kept moving forward.

Chapter 16 Ask for What You Need

1. Strategic Partners and Relational Capital matter. Do you have them? How are you using them?
2. Think differently – How can the TAG TEAM help you?
3. Who can help you find the rocks?

Chapter 17 Life is More Than Just Making a Living

1. Make memories – are you trading money for time?
2. Perfection doesn't exist; however, we are fully capable of reflection and redirection of our thoughts, choices, and deeds. How are you reflecting and redirecting?
3. What are you doing to get off your ass and create the life you want here and now?

Chapter 18 Personal Life Landmines

1. We are the result of our decisions, not our environment? What decisions do you want to make in your professional and personal life?
2. Do you see the White Knight Syndrome in your life?
3. We all have things we want to change personally and professionally. List three things you plan to improve this year.
4. Self-sabotage sinks more businesses and relationships. What action(s) are you taking when you spot something that is not right?

Chapter 19 How Did We Get Here

1. The impact of culturalization on males – Toxic masculinity. Name three things you saw growing up that re-enforced toxic masculinity?
2. The impact of culturalization on females – Cult of Domesticity. Name three things you saw growing up that re-enforced the cult of domesticity?

3. What do you believe is the most important legislation that was passed to level the playing field? What is still needed?

4. Gender roles and stereotypes are often unconscious biases. Which stereotypes do you see at work, at home, with friends?

Chapter 20 Leave Work at Work

1. How is the job taking over your life creeping up on you?

2. Being present matters – are you fully engaged at home? What can you do better?

3. Make time for family – what activities are planned with the family? List two actual plans (post-Covid), not spur-of-the-moment things.

4. Professional success is not worth the price of a shattered life. What lines will you not cross?

Chapter 21 Dialogue Requires Deep Listening

1. Are you actively listening to your spouse and children? Write down their greatest hope and fear.

2. Grand gestures are nice, but the consistency of word and deed mean far more. What things are you doing so people in your personal relationship feel special?

3. People aren't mind readers. Do you say what you mean, or do you leave things open for interpretation? List an occasion where your lack of clarity created an issue.

4. Do you and your spouse/partner Fight Fair? List your ground rules. Do you stay on topic? Do you pull in past events?

Chapter 22 Accountability in our Personal Relationships

1. The common denominator is your personal relationship failures is you. What steps are you taking to reflect and redirect your thoughts, words, and actions?

Addendum I The TAG TEAM

1. We have the skills, knowledge, and contacts. What is stopping you from getting what you want?

2. How will the TAG TEAM process help your organization?

3. If you are serious, take the 1st step. Have you submitted the TAG TEAM application?

Addendum II The Recommended Process

1. If not now – then when? What fear is preventing you from action?

2. Following the old model will likely result in failure. What new disruptive and innovative programs are you implementing? Do you know how to implement them? Have you people been there and done that?

Business and Personal Secrets for Avoiding Relationship Landmines

Courage is the commitment to begin without any guarantee of success.

Johann Wolfgang Von Goethe

Martha Beck wrote, "How we do anything is the way we do everything." Try as we may, it is impossible to separate our business/professional life from our personal life. If we are having problems in one area, problems will occur in the other. How we handle and manage any situation, challenge, or experience in our life is probably how we handle all of them. Landmines are everywhere. Now you can identify and avoid the landmines.

There is a Secret to avoiding personal and professional landmines. As a former CEO and business owner, I stepped on several business and personal landmines. I learned how to identify and avoid them going forward. I am sharing the secrets I learned with you.

For any business or personal relationship to succeed, both parties must be one hundred percent committed. No if, ands, or buts. Starting any relationship is not for the faint of heart. It takes courage to reach out. We open ourselves to rejection and disappointment as we hope to find something of lasting value. Taking the first step is both exciting and terrifying. Is it exciting in that where will this new adventure lead? Will this finally be the answer to my hopes and dreams? Terrifying as we consider how well do I know this company or person? Is what I am being told fact or fiction? Is what we both want really aligned? Are they responsible? Do they talk a good game but have no follow-through? Can I trust them?

Trust is the cornerstone for business and personal relationships. I learned long ago that you can buy someone's presence, time, and participation. You cannot buy their loyalty, trust, dedication, and commitment. You have to earn these things. You have to treasure and protect them. Constant and continuous dialogue will maintain and strengthen trust. Dhar Mann wrote:

Trust Takes Years To Build, Seconds To Break, and Forever To Repair

Issuing ultimatums in business or personal relationships like, "If I don't get this, then I am leaving" or "If this does not occur by X date, then we should both go our separate ways" rarely works well. The other party may call your bluff, then what? Are you really prepared to end the relationship? The other party may counter with what about in X more years. Pressure and guilt are a poor basis for building or sustaining a relationship. The person who is being pressured or guilted may initially agree but will do so resentfully. That resentment will, in time, raise its ugly head in the future. One party is no longer one hundred percent engaged. Ultimatums chip away at trust.

Someone asked me, "So how do I know if I am one hundred percent in?" Well, if you have to ask that question, you're not. You can't have one foot on the dock and the other in the boat. Either get in the boat or stay out altogether. I think we can safely say that for a business or personal relationship to not only survive but to thrive, both parties must be in one hundred percent.

There are many more business and personal landmines discussed throughout this book. As I said at the beginning of this introduction, it is impossible to separate our business/professional life from our personal life. Both sides impact who we are and how we do what we do. Far too often, we neglect or overlook one side. That is when the landmine explodes, and our entire life is affected.

Each chapter has discussion questions, and I have included a workbook for a deeper dive to discuss the Business and Personal Secrets for Avoiding Relationship Landmines. Use them with your team and family, or have me come in to facilitate the workbook with you.

About the Author

Long time CEO and Business Owner, Speaker, Author, Business Advisor, Roku TV Show Host

Frank Zaccari is a best-selling author who has written six books based on life-altering events. *Business Secrets for Walking on Water* is the first of a three-book series. An accomplished speaker, Frank teaches aspiring entrepreneurs at Arizona State University, is a mentor with the Veterans Treatment Court, and a mentor and judge with the University of California Entrepreneurship Academy. His International *Voice America* radio show, *Life Altering Events,* recently moved to Roku TV and has 220,000 listeners in 42 countries.

With 30 years of expert experience as a successful executive, author, and entrepreneur, Frank teaches aspiring entrepreneurs and leaders to uncover hidden opportunities, find the connections to create solutions to business and personal challenges, and build high-performing teams to succeed.

A native of western New York, Frank Zaccari served as a medic in the U.S. Air Force, then spent over 20 years in the high-tech industry. Holding senior positions with Fortune 50 organizations and turning around small and mid-size companies, Frank brings immense knowledge of business, finance, organizational development, people, and success to his engaging spoken presentations and books.

Education

- UCLA Anderson School of Business – Management Development for Entrepreneurs Certification Program
- California State University at Sacramento – Bachelors of Science – Finance
  www.frankzaccari.com

COMING SOON

Business & Personal Secrets for Avoiding Relationship Landmines

Martha Beck wrote, "How we do anything is the way we do everything." Try as we may, it is impossible to separate our personal life from our professional life. If we are having problems in one area, problems will occur in the other. How we handle and manage any one situation, challenge or experience in our life is probably how we handle all of them. Landmines are everywhere. Now you can identify and avoid the landmines.

There is a Secret to avoiding personal and professional landmines!

Made in the USA
Coppell, TX
29 June 2021

58296812R00125